MW01073453

A q
thr
whi

*her mother frees the author from destructive patterns
of relationships and brings the book full circle, revealing a family you care about, a family continuing to
learn about love and acceptance.*

> *Elizabeth W. Garber, author of "Feasting" in
> Garrison Keillor's Good Poems for Hard Times*

*For many adult daughters, "mother love" underscores
lifelong feelings of confusion, anger and deep-seated
insecurity. In The Mother of My Invention, Patricia
Taub takes an unflinching but deeply moving look at
this troubled dynamic, and charts a course for others
through its rocky terrain.*

> *Linda Lowen, About.com
> Guide to Women's Issues*

*With acute insight and striking honesty Taub draws
an affecting portrait of her fiercely private mother
who, paradoxically, confides to "Pati" her darkest secrets. It is a thoroughly engaging, often humorous story of a complex relationship, one that will seem
achingly familiar to many.*

> *Mary Cross, author of Madonna: A Biography*

*Every page of this deeply felt memoir offers proof of
how complicated the umbilical connection is. Often it
takes decades to become truly on our own, and to
realize that our mothers were autonomous beings,
that they, too, had to make their own challenging way
through the forest.*

> *Ginnah Howard, author of Night Navigation*

The Mother of My Invention

by
PATRICIA TAUB

Patricia Taub

AUTHOR'S NOTE

Names have been changed for privacy's sake.
My own name and my mother's name are real.

ISBN 978-0-557-33158-1

ACKNOWLEDGMENTS

Clare Mead Rosen helped me to produce a far better book than I imagined possible when I handed her the first rambling draft of this memoir. A former Contributing Editor of TIME Magazine, Clare is a brilliant wordsmith, and more: she was a profound emotional support to me, especially when long-buried memories reemerged with unsettling intensity. Clare shares my zany sense of humor. Laughter carried us through many a frustrating interlude.

Additionally, I want to thank the good friends and family members who read various drafts and gave me a thumbs up. Writing a book for the first time is a little like being pregnant for the first time. As the final months drag on, you wonder if Delivery Day will ever arrive. But eventually babies are born and so are books.

CONTENTS

"A story...shows us the way out, down, or up, and for our trouble, cuts for us fine wide doors in previously blank walls, openings that lead to...love and understanding...."

Clarissa Pinkola Estés, Ph.D
Women Who Run With the Wolves

I

Christmas Approaches, 1999

In all likelihood this will be my mother's last Christmas. This past spring, on Mother's Day, of all days, she was rushed to the hospital after suddenly gasping for breath for no apparent reason. In the hall outside her hospital room, a specialist summoned by her doctor explained to my brothers and me that Mother was terminal with pulmonary fibrosis. For awhile she would be able to get around with a portable oxygen tank, but eventually her lungs would begin to shut down, leaving her too weak to leave the apartment. I stared numbly at the specialist's tie, which was emblazoned with golf clubs. He described a grim death comparable to drowning: "The patient literally suffocates, but morphine will be administered at this stage to reduce discomfort."

I wanted to scream, "The *patient*? This is my mother!" Nate and Gary, my younger brothers, pressed for more information.

Dr. Golfclubs responded, "No one can be exactly sure how much time your mother has, but she's eighty-one so I'd put my money on somewhere around a year-and-a-half. Now

I have to go." Then he turned sharply, throwing his corpulent body off-center in the process. He shuffled his feet to regain his balance. A hex on your golf game, I thought.

Three seasons have come and gone since that terrible Mother's Day. Lady Jane has fashioned herself into a professional pulmonary patient. She deftly dons and doffs her portable oxygen canister, leaving it behind on the car seat whenever she goes out to dinner, lest anyone she knows should see her with it. Mother drives herself to the hospital for her weekly rehab sessions, where she enjoys gossiping about celebrities with the jovial head nurse. At home Jane chatters non-stop on the phone. She makes short runs to the grocery store and occasionally shops at the Mall, accompanied by Carla Thomas, her wonderful housekeeper of thirty-eight years. Jane pretends that she takes Carla along to keep her company, but Mother can no longer carry packages or walk for long without requiring an arm to lean on. To the outside world Mother presents an image of a woman whose failing lungs are no more significant than a bad cold.

Generally, I, too, tend to minimize signs of Mother's decline, going along with her masquerade and zapping mental images of her death as if they were pop-up ads on the Internet. Like the ads, however, they keep coming back, especially when Mother's voice sounds weak, or when a friend asks, "How's your mother doing?"

My brothers collude in the family denial. Gary and Nate make euphemistic references to Mother's "end stage," as if they were speaking of a disembodied event. They seem so detached that we remain at arm's length from each other, making me feel isolated and lonely. Even so, I'm as powerless as they are to face the truth head on.

I decide at some point to talk to myself to make it sink in that Mother will die soon. I don't get very far. Mother's refusal to speak of her death fuels my ongoing denial. At the same time I grow frustrated. I want us to be real. I long to have a genuine conversation with my mother about her dying. This is a fantasy, I know. Mother has never really revealed herself to me, except in some patently unhealthy ways. I make a mental note to go back into therapy to sort it all out, but I know I won't do this anytime soon. It's more than I can handle right now. Based on past therapy experiences, as soon as I describe my relationship with Mother, my anger surfaces and before I know it I find myself sobbing uncontrollably. (If polled, I suspect my previous therapists would not hesitate to award me a bronze Kleenex box.)

It is impossible to have a normal conversation with Mother. Spontaneity is out; I have to choose my words carefully. Even an inno-cuous greeting like, "Hi Mother, how are you?" can be problematic. For someone who guards her privacy as zealously as Mother does, this is not a polite opener. It's an intrusion.

Whenever she perceives that I am getting too close for comfort her caustic tone sounds a familiar warning: "I'm *fine, just fine.*"

"I only ask because Carla told me you had a rough night."

"I wish Carla would mind her own business!" Mother invariably retorts. I'm not proud of myself for making her angry, or of the resentment I feel toward her after I do.

Mother's coldness triggers my old gut fears of abandonment – fears I remember from childhood and well beyond. I'll never forget a lunch date we had when I was in my early forties. I confessed to Mother, in what I thought was a diplomatic way, that I felt a lot of tension during family gatherings. She startled me by retorting, "Maybe you shouldn't visit so much, if the family upsets you the way it seems to." For all that, it was Mother herself who had burdened me with some devastating family secrets when I was growing up. It was not the kind of intimacy I craved.

When it becomes apparent that Mother won't be up to flying to Milwaukee to spend Christmas with Gary and his wife, Joan --

something she's done for the past ten years --
I offer to come to Harrisburg for the holidays
with my two grown sons, Sam and
Adam. I know the boys will be fine with this
plan because they have a completely different
relationship with their grandmother than
I do. They've rarely experienced her hyper-
controlling behavior. To Sam and Adam, their
grandmother is always caring, funny and
charmingly eccentric.

Gary and Nate sound relieved when
I tell them I'll spend Christmas with Jane.
Even though they are deferential around her,
Mother's narcissism drives them nuts. They
make dark comedy out of it. Recently Nate
joked: "Mother's going to die from talking
about herself: her lungs don't have the capac-
ity for around-the-clock chatter."

I share my brothers' frustration, and, like
them, I don't challenge Mother directly.
Sometimes I guiltily pine for my father's way
of containing Mother. He would listen to her
rattle on for just so long, then he'd blow: "For
God's sake Jane, can't you stop talking for
one minute?" This always worked. She'd instantly shut up.

My father could be verbally abusive. He
intimidated Mother. He intimidated all of us,
in fact. As a feminist I should have resented
his treatment of my mother, but my relief at
getting a break from her self-centered prattle

made me rationalize my father's callous, un-caring words.

Right after Thanksgiving Nate and Gary surprise me by announcing they'll be bring-ing their families to Harrisburg for Christmas after all. They've booked rooms in the Mar-riott across the street from Mother's apart-ment building. For all their stiff-upper-lip be-havior, it is clear that they've come to grips with the high probability that the Christmas of 1999 will be Mother's last. I'm actually looking forward to being with my mother this year. She's always romanticized the holidays. Like her, I lose myself in the magical fantasy of Christmas, going all out decorating, buying gifts and entertaining.

Today when we talk on the phone Mother obsesses about things she can no longer control. Her frustration is understand-able, and it shows. She worries that Carla won't pick out a good tree, or that she won't find any "homemade" cookies now that Annie George, the baker she relies on, has retired. Mother frets that grandson Mark will do an inferior job stringing the lights. Last year he placed all the lights on the top half of the tree, creating the illusion of a tree in space.

Her concerns are almost comical at times, but I suppress the urge to laugh. In-stead, I try to allay her anxiety. An idea comes to me: "Mother, why don't you call Simon (her favorite florist) and ask him to take charge of all the decorating? Just like all those society matrons in New York do." I've said exactly the right thing. Mother loves to think of herself as the Brooke Astor of Harrisburg.

Last summer Mother let me in on what her big Christmas present was going to be to Gary, Nate and me. She would create a personal album for each of us, assembling photos, letters we wrote as kids, newspaper clippings of our accomplishments, and other bits of memorabilia. On the face of it that is a very thoughtful gift, especially under the circumstances. An outsider might say, "How touching that your dying mother wanted to leave each of her children a personal memory book made with her very own arthritic hands." But such scrapbooks are Mother's trademarks. I've received similar ones for every milestone birthday, and in each one half of the book is filled with pictures of her and Dad, most of them taken during one of their stylish excursions abroad. On one page they might be seen relaxing in a hotel suite in Mayfair, or waving as they disembark from a plane in Beijing. On the next, they might be dining at a four star restaurant in San Francisco or New York. Inevitably the photos take us back home, usually to showcase -- from every possible angle -- Mother's latest redecorating efforts. To me, the scrapbooks are just one more exercise in narcissism.

I was married at twenty-two and divorced at forty-two. In the fourteen years since then I've often been alone for Christmas, but I've always had a tree. This will be my first year without one. To compensate, I buy a potted Norfolk pine, which I decorate and place in a copper container I ordered online from Martha Stewart. I also hang a large Della Robbia wreath on the front door and, as usual, set out Nana's porcelain angel collection and the Mercury Glass reindeers Mother gave me when she co-owned an antique store in Harrisburg.

What do you buy for your mother when it might be her last Christmas on earth? The last time she'll hold up a new sweater to take in its style; the last time she'll fake admiration for a gift she doesn't want; the last time she'll be moved by the tender gift of a special family photo; or chuckle at a present from a grandchild, like the pillow that declared "I Love My Hip Grandmother."

I readily get into the rhythm of shopping for Mother, spending way more than I should on all sorts of things that I know she'd love, as if I must pack all the future Christmases she will never know into this one.

The night before I leave for Harrisburg, I light some votive candles, insert the Nutcracker CD, pour myself a glass of red wine and sink into the sofa. Before I know it, I am in tears. I will miss Mother. She's my only surviving parent, the last bulwark between me and my own mortality.

My thoughts stray to Peter, my erstwhile demon lover. We broke up yet again this past September. Mother was always there for me whenever my relationship with Peter crashed. She was always able to put herself aside and devote herself to me, boosting my spirits and telling me I deserve better than Peter with his quick-change charm, romancing me one day and being cruel the next.

I've often wondered whether the intensity Mother has always brought to her "Peter lectures" was influenced by her own relationship to Dad, who thought nothing of putting Mother down in public, especially when he'd had a few martinis. One of his favorite derisions took the form of a biting left-handed compliment: "Jane, you're not as dumb as you look" -- offered whenever Mother said something insightful.

The morning of December twenty-second I pack my Honda CRV with my suitcase, presents, and a few gourmet foods to accompany the cocktail hour—a wheel of Brie, some pate, spinach dip—and a small crate of clementines. At the last minute I decide against the camcorder. I remember how uncomfortable Dad was during his last Thanksgiving, when we videotaped the entire occasion. Rather than make Mother self-conscious, I'll have to rely on my memory of this holiday.

The drive from Syracuse to Harrisburg takes about four hours if I keep the cruise control at seventy-five and limit my pit stops. The roads are dry. There has not yet been a major snowstorm this winter; the radio announces there's only a slim chance Harrisburg will see a white Christmas. Two hours into my journey I'm at the base of the Pocono Mountains, which provide a welcome diversion from the flat topography around Syracuse. The Poconos hold a mixed bag of memories for me: I attended an oppressive girls' summer camp there from the time I was ten until I turned thirteen; the Poconos are also where Dad took us to hear Duke Ellington; and where, in the summer of 1964, I secretly camped with my future husband.

On the outskirts of Harrisburg, I nostalgically take in the gray fieldstone farmhouses; pass signs for the Amish country and Hershey Park. Finally I make the turn-off for the old family house, feeling the need to see it before I go on to Mother's new apartment on the riverfront. My stomach constricts in anticipation when I am a block away from 2410 Melrose Road. My brothers tell me they never drive past "2410." I can't stay away. This time the appearance of my childhood home saddens me even more than the last time I drove by. There are broken fence slats; the shrubbery is overgrown and an artificial wreath on the front door appears to be a cheap grocery store purchase—a far cry from the exquisite wreaths Mother used to create out of dried hydrangeas or fresh holly.

I was well into adulthood before I could see the house for what it was, instead of through the lens of Mother's elaborate fantasies. It was just a nice upper-middle-class 1950s Cape Cod, with a bay window in front, a small, well-landscaped yard, a split rail fence, and a colonial lamppost. But to Mother our house deserved a spread in Better Homes and Gardens.

I close my eyes to shutter out the present, recalling the Christmases of my childhood. I remember how, as soon as it got dark, I would switch on the electric candles in the front windows. In the kitchen I would help Nana make sand tarts. Down in the basement Nana and I would wrap gifts on the laundry table. I could never get the hang of making a good bow. Why do I associate Christmas with Nana and not Mother? Where was Mother during this time?

I stare at the house, as if it can give me answers. But the house resists my inquiries. Every window shade is drawn, mocking me: "Get on with your life. You won't find the key to your childhood's mysteries here."

I pull away from the old neighborhood and drive down Market Street, passing the place where the farmer's market once was. Mother and I used to buy vegetables and flowers there on Saturdays. The market long ago gave way to a Kentucky Fried Chicken franchise, where low-income, mostly black, residents of the nearby row houses come for take-out. The middle class whites who used to live here decamped years ago to the suburbs. A little farther on, the bakery where Mother used to purchase coconut layer cakes is boarded up, as is Harry's, once a popular college hangout where students came for draft beer and steamed clams. Further on I pass a graffiti-covered building that is now sealed off. I briefly endured ballet classes there. The only inhabited buildings I see have seedy exteriors -- a mini-mart, a liquor store, a gas station and a video store.

As I approach Mother's apartment building on Front Street, the scene changes entirely. Expensively renovated town houses stretch for blocks and blocks along the Susquehanna River. White Christmas lights sparkle from the branches of newly planted trees gracing the riverbank. I turn into the parking lot behind Mother's building, suddenly feeling old and bewildered. Where did all the decades go?

Mother won the admiration of her friends four years ago, when, only a year after Dad's death, she matter-of-factly sold the family home of forty-five years and moved to an apartment downtown. Emma Green, Mother's business partner in the antique store for ten years, pronounced Jane "a very brave woman," for making the move. I didn't find

Mother's decision so courageous. She had plenty of money to indulge her fantasy of being Harrisburg's reigning grande dame. It wasn't as if she was a widow on a fixed income and needed to downsize to save dough. Mother didn't rent one apartment, but two, wearing down the building's owner until he gave her permission to knock down the walls so that she could create the look of a spacious Park Avenue apartment.

During our phone chats Mother regularly pats herself on the back for this architectural achievement, telling me that so-and-so (her latest visitor) "was just here and said, 'I feel like I'm in a New York City penthouse!' No one in Harrisburg has an apartment like this, Pati!"

Now Fate has handed Mother a cruel card: a terminal illness, less than four years after she has moved into her dream apartment. My heart aches to know that after fifty-four years of accommodating a domineering husband, Mother's had so little time to enjoy her new life. After Dad was gone, she relished doing whatever she wanted to, whenever she wanted to. She began to stay up past midnight, surfing TV channels or playing Frank Sinatra CDs; she stocked the fridge with champagne splits and kept her pockets supplied with Hershey kisses. Mother radiates her new happiness, repeatedly telling me, "I just love my apartment." To me this was code for: *I love my new life. I'm finally out from under your father's big thumb.*

But now it's time for me to get out of the car and go up to Jane's apartment. I've rummaged through enough memories for one day.

II

A Brush With Intimacy

I quietly let myself into the apartment and go straight to the kitchen. Carla is filling a plastic bag with items Mother has set aside for her to take home: some tree ornaments, a tin of Christmas cookies and a jar of spaghetti sauce with a label that reads "From the Kitchen of Judith Danforth." Mother automatically rejects anything this friend gives her, insisting that Judith's food is "too heavy." I think the real reason is that Judith gets on her nerves. Mother craves attention, but it has to be at arm's length, especially when it comes to people like Judith, who stand uncomfortably close when they talk to you, as if the two of you are sharing the last spot in a crowded elevator. I also suspect that Judith's well-meant but cloying compliments make Mother uncomfortable: "Your Mother is one of the most beautiful people I know. She's just perfection in everything she does."

I whisper to Carla, "How's Mother?" Every word spoken in the kitchen is audible in Mother's bedroom.

Carla whispers back, "She just dozed off."

I help Carla with her coat and she gives me a hug before loading the bulging bag of goodies onto one arm and her cracked leather pocketbook onto the other. I can always count on Carla for a good hug. I wish her well, and shut the door quietly behind her.

After almost four decades as Mother's housekeeper, Carla is an expert at reading Jane and handling her moods. Thus, she knows that Mother wants her to relay terse, positive health reports to me and Gary and Nate, nothing to cause concern. It wasn't until after Dad died that I began to realize how much Carla perceives and how wise she is. She once confided to me, "Your Mother tells everyone she's 'independent' so they won't get too close to her. She's very private and very fragile."

I tiptoe toward Mother's room. My throat tightens. I don't want to walk in on her when she looks terrible. I'm afraid she'll display worsened symptoms that I won't be able to handle. From the open door I see her sleeping in her La-Z-Boy, which is upholstered in white calico patterned with pastel seashells. Everything else in her room is pure white: the walls, the wicker bed frame, the white organdy bedspread, the dressers and lamps, her antique wicker trunk and a round glass-topped wrought iron table. As I gaze around the room, it occurs to me what a soothing thing it must be to die in an all-white room. I read somewhere that white, not black, is the color of death in many cultures.

Mother is wearing the green velvet robe I gave her last Christmas. Even in sleep her body retains a kind of tension; her arms extend rigidly along her sides. Yet she is still pretty at eighty-one. She was always the standout beauty among Mother and Dad's friends, with her dark hair and large brown eyes, her luminous skin, full breasts and slim legs. Photos from the Fifties and Sixties show Mother and Dad at cocktail parties, at country club dances, at pool parties and at Christmas galas. In each picture Mother's beauty eclipses everyone else's. Despite her weakened state now, she still attends to her daily beauty routine, making sure her night cream is applied and her wavy (now dyed-brown) hair is brushed.

I stand listening to her raspy breathing for a few moments, and then, as if she feels my presence, Mother wakes up and smiles at me, "Oh, it's Pati. When did you get here?"

"Just a few minutes ago," I answer. I kiss her cheek and embrace her thin frame gingerly. When did she get so small? I feel as if she might break if I hug her too hard.

I watch Jane watching me and realize she's forgotten to deliver her usual motherly appraisal of me. Or is she still pondering? What will it be this time? My clothes, my weight, my hair? Her gaze settles on my head: "Pati, do you like your hair that way?"

"Not particularly. I got a bad perm. It's growing out."

"I wish you'd stop experimenting with your hair and settle on one becoming style, like Jackie Kennedy. She never changed her hairstyle."

"Mother, this perm has to grow out; then my hair will look better." For Christ's sake, I think to myself, the last thing I want is a Jackie-do.

"Well, why didn't you do something about it for Christmas?"

"Short of a buzz cut, there's nothing I can do. I told you it has to grow out. Can we talk about something else besides my hair?"

"You don't have to get smart with me. It's just that you're so attractive. Have you thought about changing hairdressers? Joan's hair always looks nice; too bad she lives in Milwaukee, or you could go to her hairdresser."

I could absolutely pop at this moment, but that would not be a good start to my Christmas visit. So I bite my lip and change the subject. I know from a recent phone chat that Mother is not entirely happy with what Simon, the floral *artiste,* has done to the apartment, so it isn't hard to divert her to that topic.

Her first complaint is about the tree. "Why did Simon use such large Christmas balls?" she says.

"I noticed that when I came in. They look like small planets."

This makes Mother laugh. She manages to rise in order to tour me through the apartment to point out Simon's other mistakes. She walks from room to room with twin oxygen tubes trailing from her nostrils. They meet beneath her chin, where they merge into a single line leading to a bulky oxygen cylinder that stands in the hall outside her bedroom. (This strategic location, chosen by Mother, and the extra-long tether she insists on having, allow her to navigate through her bedroom, the kitchen, the sitting room and the den without having to move the canister even once. The limitation of this arrangement is that the lengthy oxygen line tends to tangle itself around her ankle or get hooked on furniture.)

Mother is upset with the candles on the coffee table: they are supposed to evoke silvery fir trees but Mother thinks they are tacky. I offer to call Simon and have them exchanged.

"No, you can't do that. We'll just live with them." Mother has never been able to challenge anyone outside the family, even when she's paying someone to please her. She makes excuses to cover her dissatisfaction. If she doesn't finish her meal in a restaurant, she'll explain to the waiter, who couldn't care less, "The food was delicious, but I just don't have much of an appetite tonight." Once outside, she'll rail on about how horrid the meal was! My favorite of all her camouflages is the line she uses when we enter a shop and instantly realize it doesn't have the sorts of things we like. Instead of just leaving, Mother feels she owes an explanation to the nearest clerk within earshot: "Everything here is so beautiful, but we just remembered we're late for an appointment."

After Mother checks off Simon's remaining faux pas -- the hall centerpiece shouldn't be silver and blue, but red and green; the window wreaths are hung too high -- I suggest that we turn on the tree lights, sit down and have a glass of wine. Mother agrees. Complaining takes energy and she's run out of it.

Once lit, the tree transforms the room, projecting feathery branches onto the walls and ceiling. The effect is both pleasing and calming. Mother relaxes. "I'm glad you're here," she says. I tell her I'll correct Simon's mistakes tomorrow and purchase fresh flowers for the dining room table. More than anyone in the family, I know just how Mother likes things to look.

For some time there's been a whispering concern in the family about Mother's increasingly strong body odor. Because she's been unwilling to have help with personal hygiene but is too weak to adequately take care of herself, this was bound to happen. No one has had the nerve to mention it to her, but, on the morning of December twenty-fourth, a few hours before the first members of the family are due, I summon the courage to confront her. My stomach turns over in anticipation of offending Mother, but I proceed anyway, knowing that the alternative will embarrass her even more.

Taking a deep breath, I blurt it out, "Mother, I don't know how to say this tactfully, so I'll just tell you: I've noticed you have body odor. I don't want you to be embarrassed by it, that's why I think you should shower. I'll be glad to help you."

Mother is appalled. "What! I have body odor?"

"Yes, I'm afraid so. Why don't you let me help you take a shower?" It's one of those rare occasions when Mother is speechless. Her small panic moves me. Mother's privacy is extreme when it comes to her body, yet she's trapped. Looking anxious, she consents, then, recovering her defenses, adds, "OK, let's make it quick. Help me into the shower and I'll do the rest."

I release the zipper that runs down the front of Mother's robe. She holds onto me as she steps over it, cautiously lifting one leg after the other and then stepping into her tub shower. I am able to adjust the rubber mat just before her feet land on it. I try not to stare but I haven't seen Mother totally naked for longer than I can remember. She's skinny to the point of emaciation. Her formerly full breasts have turned into limp balloons. She has virtually no pubic hair. Mother's old lady body takes me aback. I wish it would go away, replaced by the voluptuous Mother of my childhood.

Mother notices my staring. Her discomfort turns to irritability. "Pati, give me my washcloth and pull the curtain!"

I protest, for fear she'll fall. "Mother, why don't you let me wash your back first?"

Without speaking, Mother turns, faces the shower, and offers her back. I rub the Ivory soap-lathered washcloth up and down her bony spine and rib cage. I'm half relieved when Mother declines my offer to wash her any further.

But there's one aspect of her body odor that has to be addressed. It takes all the gumption I've got to speak. "Mother, forgive me, but you really need to wash your crotch."

Annoyed, she complies superficially, but I'm thankful for this much, wanting the moment to be over as much as she does.

After she's finished and out of the tub she lets me towel her back and legs, but insists on drying the rest of her body herself. Her scaly legs need attention. "Mother, before you put on your stockings, let me apply some lotion to your legs." I root around in the medicine cabinet before she can say no, announcing, "Here's a bottle of Nivea."

"Oh, I like Nivea. All right, you can put some on my legs. Let me get on my underwear first. Can you fetch a bra and underpants from my top right hand drawer?" I oblige, producing a Maidenform that looks like a relic from the 1950s, along with yellowing nylon underpants that look like they'd fit someone twice her size.

I modestly hand them to Mother through a crack in the bathroom door and tell her, "When you're ready, come sit on the bed so I can rub your legs with Nivea." Her spindly limbs with their protruding blue veins do not look as if they can absorb more than a tablespoon of the lotion. Nevertheless I apply it generously and slowly rub it in.

This gentle massage helps her relax, prompting a rare personal confession: "Pati, no one has touched me like this for a very long time."

I want to cry. I want to hug her and kiss away all the pain in her past -- from her difficult childhood to this day. But I don't dare. I'm lucky to have gotten this far. Feebly, I utter, "Well, maybe I can do this again tomorrow."

Mother smiles in response. How can I be furious with my dying mother one minute and heart-broken for her the next? Jane emphatically waves me out of the room so that she can dress. Our sweet brush with intimacy is over.

* * *

Repelling all efforts to slow her down, Mother continues to orchestrate the Christmas festivities as she always has and to dominate every conversation. She refuses to rest when it's obvious that she's fatigued. The weaker she feels the bossier she gets. It's pretty clear that her last days on earth are going to go her way or no way.

Sam and Adam had seen Mom-Mom at Thanksgiving and were prepared for the way she looks now, but the other grandchildren hadn't seen her since last summer and were taken aback by their grandmother's deterioration. Several times I notice them looking at Mother with serious faces. Nate's daughter, Dora, urgently asks me to convince Mother to use her oxygen regularly. I smile tenderly at Dora and remind her of her grandmother's stubborn nature.

Two camps emerge within the family. The older generation -- my brothers and I and their wives, all of us in our fifties, comprise the "Jane is Driving Us Nuts" faction. The grandchildren, all in their twenties and thirties, make up the "Mom-Mom is Really Cool" faction.

Mother wins points from them for being an ardent fan of the Phillies baseball team and Penn State's football team, the Nittany Lions. Her knowledge of sports is impressive. Unlike guy fans, who cuss, shout and bang their fists when their teams let them down, Mother responds to a bad play with a lady-like scolding: "Joe Paterno (Penn State's coach) knows better than to kick when his team is on the forty-five yard line."

Mother's fast driving has always contributed to her "cool granny" image. In better days she used to whip expertly in and out of alleys to avoid traffic lights. When she'd arrive at her destination -- the supermarket, for example -- she'd glance at her watch and announce, "We shaved six minutes off our time!"

There have been plenty of occasions when the grandchildren have laughed *at* Mother, not *with* her, but even then she scores extra points because of the endearingly humorous outcomes. A committed clipper of newspaper articles, Mother often sends articles to her grandchildren to document a concern, like the time she mailed Sam a New York Times story about the high crime rate in Chicago, urging him not to go out at night.

Her birthday greetings are sometimes bizarrely humorous without intending to be. One year she mailed to Adam, who lives in LA, a card featuring a good-looking young black man on a beach. "This reminded me of you," she wrote. Mother thought it was a white guy with a deep tan like the one her California grandson has.

III

Doctors, Lovers and Madmen

This is a winter of discontent if ever there was one, yet I find my hopes rising as the months go on. Mother has turned out to be a fighter, just as Dad was. He lived two years longer than his doctors predicted.

I arrive for a visit in early Spring at daffodil time. The apartment is eerily quiet. I'm accustomed to hearing Mother on the phone, or having her call out to me when she hears the door open. I'm tempted to call her name, but don't want to disturb her if she's sleeping. I check her bedroom. She's not there. I follow her oxygen tube, which leads to the den. There, alongside the open closet door, I find Mother slumped over on the floor! Her navy blue cardigan droops off one shoulder. Her glasses lie on the carpet some distance away. Her gray flannel skirt is hiked up, exposing her right knee, which is badly bruised and cut. Mother is cradling her knee in her hands and whimpering softly from the pain. I try not to show alarm. She raises her head and looks up at me. Her eyes register a mixture of panic and relief. I don't want to increase her anxiety by appearing flustered. Bending over her, lowering my voice, I ask, "Mother, what happened?"

In spite of her discomfort, she's feisty: "What do you think happened? I fell. Just help me up. I'll be alright once I sit down and get some ice on my leg."

Mother's snappy tone causes me to lose my cool. In a voice coated with irritation I respond, "What if I hadn't arrived just now? If you had agreed to using a med alert you could have called for help."

She glares at me and responds curtly, "I would have managed somehow. Don't talk to me right now about a safety gadget! Just help me up."

I assist her into one of the room's pair of leather club chairs and head for the kitchen to make an ice pack, endeavoring to use this little break to talk myself out of saying something I might regret. Returning to the den with cracked ice wrapped inside a clean dishcloth, I find Mother breathing heavily. She refuses my assistance in adjusting her oxygen tubes. Once she's got them in place in her nostrils, she reaches out for the ice pack and places it gingerly on her knee. As she shifts her position her skirt catches, revealing older bruises on her other leg. Clearly she has been falling more than any of us realized.

I'm entering the zone where Mother usually wins, but I have to know what's at stake, so I press on, feeling like Alice confronting the Queen of Hearts. "Mother, I know that you're taking more spills than before. Do you realize that if this continues, you could seriously hurt yourself? If you're totally opposed to a med alert, what about a cane or even a walker?" I immediately regret the walker reference.

With an adrenaline surge, Mother barks, "I will *never* use a walker -- or a cane for that matter! I just have to pace myself to avoid falling." From past experience I know not to press the argument because if I do Mother will pull one of her hyperventilating stunts or clutch her chest in a fake gesture of pain.

There are other new signs of distress: Mother's oxygen canister is turned up a notch from where it was the last time I visited her. She's lost weight, as well. Her clothes hang off of her. I won't bring any of this up with Mother, but I will mention it to my brothers.

I suggest one of Mother's favorite dishes for dinner: crab cakes from Inn 22. I phone for a take-out order and bring the food back to a more relaxed Jane, who smiles appreciatively from her chair, where I've set her up with a TV table. She is trying as hard as I am to get us back on an even keel, feigning enthusiasm as I lift the perfectly fried crab cakes from their Styrofoam container and place them on her dinner plate. After only a few microscopic bites, she explains in an exhausted voice, "I'm sorry, Pati, but I can't finish my dinner. I haven't had much of an appetite lately."

While we're watching Antiques Roadshow on PBS I ask Mother when her next appointment is with Dr. Rowen. She tells me it's this coming Monday. I offer to stay an extra day to take her to her appointment, figuring it will give me a chance to broach the subject of her falls and weight loss. I'm hoping Rowen will back me up and convince Mother that she really does need a "safety gadget" now.

To my surprise Mother readily accepts my offer to go with her to the doctor, but I quickly realize that it's not my moral support she's interested in. Rather, she suggests that I can be more assertive than Carla in appealing to the receptionist to shorten Mother's waiting time. I nod my head in recognition. Mother is counting on me to employ the pushy charm I learned from her.

Once Mother is in bed for the night I phone Gary and then Nate, describing her fall and the evidence of past falls. They are relieved that I will accompany Mother to Dr. Rowen's office, but neither brother thinks there's much of a chance that he can convince her to use a med alert.

As I lie awake in bed reviewing my conversations with my brothers, it seems apparent to me that they have resigned themselves to Mother's determination to die on her own terms. Why am I unable to do the same? Am

I just stubborn, like Mother? No, I tell myself. A med alert could save her from dying alone from a fall, or having to spend the little time she has left being an invalid in a nursing home. The panic I saw in her eyes when I entered the den today told me she doesn't want that, either.

When it's time for us to depart for Dr. Rowen's office Mother does not insist on driving, unlike prior times. She hands over the car keys to me. As I help her into her minivan, I notice some new dents on the rear passenger side. We drive in solemn silence to Rowen's office. Mother's characteristic chatter is conspicuously absent.

Less than ten minutes after we are seated in Dr. Rowen's crowded waiting room, Mother prods her lady-in-waiting into action, whispering impatiently to me, "Pati, do something. Get me back there." It feels premature to hassle the receptionist, but Mother won't buy this, retorting, "We could be here all day. Go tell the receptionist I have a lot of things to do and have to be seen right away."

I comply. The receptionist smiles across the room at Mother and informs me that we can wait in the hall on the other side of the waiting room's double doors. Mother and I take our positions on folding chairs facing the interior nurse's station. Mother scans a tabloid she's found on the table beside her, registering outrage at Dolly Parton's thundering breasts.

After twenty-five minutes we're escorted into an examining room where we wait another fifteen minutes before Dr. Rowen enters. He waddles over (Nate calls him "the penguin") to where Jane lies on the examining table, then takes her hand and continues to hold it as he describes an art auction he attended the past weekend.

This is more than I can take. We're not here for a social visit. I interrupt: "Dr. Rowen, I'm very concerned about Mother. She's falling a lot lately. She doesn't have much of an appetite, and as you can see, she's lost weight." Mother turns her head in my direction. Her eyes narrow in disapproval. If she were a queen she'd now be thrusting a finger toward the door to dismiss me as her lady-in-waiting.

Dr. Rowen lets go of Mother's hand and appraises her tiny frame, "Jane, you do look thinner. Step up on the scale and we'll weigh you." He helps Mother onto the platform and slides the brass weights back and forth on the bobbing arm of the scale until they rest at one hundred and four pounds. "Have you been drinking Ensure every day as I recommended?"

I'm encouraged. Finally, Dr. Rowen is acting like a doctor.

Mother coyly replies, "Oh Ken, I just don't like the way it tastes." She steps off the scale, casting a flirtatious smile while Rowen assists her back to the examining table.

Clearly disarmed, Dr. Rowen does his best to make his point to Mother without upsetting her. He speaks softly, "Jane, we have to build you up. You'll have to try to drink two cans of Ensure every day. And now that Pati's here, maybe she can cook your favorite dishes."

Since I've been named, I respond, "That didn't work this weekend. Whatever I made, Mother didn't have an appetite for."

Mother becomes defensive, "It's not that I don't like Pati's cooking. For some reason I haven't been hungry. If I have to, I can make myself drink Ensure."

Mother's eyes harden as she casts me a warning glance. She employs a familiar maneuver: "Now can we talk about something else?" She goes on to tell Dr. Rowen that her children don't think she should drive to Chautauqua this summer, "but I feel perfectly capable of making the drive. Don't you agree?"

"Is our old friend Ellen going with you again?"

"Yes, she is."

Rowen looks at me: "Your Mother should be fine if Ellen is with her."

What? Ellen is ninety, can barely walk, and has such a weak, scratchy voice that her cries for help would never be heard. Neither she nor Mother uses a cell phone. Nevertheless, I recognize the futility of arguing my case any further. Jane wins the day. Again.

After Mother is asleep that night, I curl up on the living room sofa with a glass of white wine and begin to mull old memories, particularly conversations with Aunt Gerda, the widow of my mother's twin brother, Paul, who died two years ago. Jane and Gerda met as teenagers and belonged to the same high school sorority. It was Mother who introduced Gerda to Paul.

Aunt Gerda is our family's Deep Throat. She used to take me into her confidence late in the evening, phoning after she'd downed one too many glasses of Scotch. On one of those nights when I happened to answer the phone, Aunt Gerda revealed that Mother and Dr. Rowen had once had an affair. No doubt it was payback for Dad's legion of lovers over the years: airline hostesses, secretaries, even call girls.

It was Mother herself, however, who told me about an affair she'd had with a family friend named Dan. I'll never forget the day she told me. It was one of those hot, humid Saturdays in August. Lenny and I and the boys were spending the weekend in Harrisburg with my parents. I was reading in a lounge chair next to Dad, who was working on his Cary Grant tan. Lenny and Sam and Adam were happily swimming in the backyard pool. When I looked up from my book I could see Mother beckoning to me from the kitchen window. I went inside. She said she had something to show me. I followed her upstairs, where she ushered me into her bedroom and closed the door.

From experience I knew not to sit on the bed lest I muss up the spread. I took a seat on an upholstered bench as Mother opened her top dresser drawer and reached into the back. She turned to face me holding a Georg Jensen jewelry box, which she carefully opened, revealing a stunning sterling silver cuff bracelet. "I want you to have this. It's a gift from Dan Gardner, but I can't keep it because your father would be suspicious."

"Mother, it's beautiful. But why would Dan Gardner give you such an expensive gift?"

Smiling knowingly, Mother replied, "We're very good friends."

To which I blurted out, "Mother, are you sleeping with him?"

Assuming the aspect of a French film actress, Mother gave me a telling look, "What do you think?"

That response set off all sorts of Freudian bells for me. "My mother is having sex with another man! My mother is having sex, period. Egad!"

Overcome by disturbing images, I stared at the wall, cringing inside. Not knowing what to say, I got up and left Mother's bedroom with the contraband bracelet concealed in my beach towel.

Over the next nine months, whenever Mother visited us in Oneonta, or we made a trip to Harrisburg, she smuggled additional Dan Gardner gifts to me. In an attempt to extricate myself from my mother's secret love life, I transferred my unwelcome booty to my friend Sally. Besides the silver bracelet, Sally came into the possession of a bottle of Chanel No. 5 perfume, a luxurious silk scarf, and an antique music box.

When Mother finally ended her affair with Dan rather than leave Dad, as her lover had pressed her to do, Sally's lucky streak came to an end. In the ensuing months, whenever Sally and I got together, she would teasingly inquire if Mother had a new boyfriend yet.

I didn't really blame Mother for having an affair. While Dad's gifts were just as extravagant as Dan's, Dad didn't give her the attention and affection Dan did.

My father was an angry man, quick to take out his everyday tensions on Mother. He would yell at her for no apparent reason, frequently slamming doors as he stormed out of the house, sometimes halfway through a family dinner.

My brothers and I caught a good share of Dad's rage, too. He whacked us with what he called his "black stick," a small flat paddle that Dad bought and painted black to render it even more intimidating. I began hiding it from him when I was about seven. By the time I was eleven or twelve, and unlike my brothers, I began to challenge my father verbally. A big mistake: he'd grab my arms so tightly that his fingers sometimes left bruise marks. Once he even banged my head against the kitchen wall, as Mother cried and begged him to stop. Not long afterward, Dad stopped hitting us for good.

Mother said something to me about Peter at breakfast this morning that now makes me wonder: am I a masochist like she is, putting up with men who treat me poorly? While Mother didn't recognize all the ways Dad mistreated her, she was a regular Miss Marple when it came to her daughter's love life. This morning I was casually sipping my coffee when she asked out-of-the-blue, "What's going on with you and Peter? I thought you broke it off with him, but it sounded like you were talking with him last night on the phone."

I choked on my toast. How could she have heard me? I'd been careful to wait a full hour after Mother went to bed before I phoned him. Since I'd been caught, I had no choice but to confess. "You're right, I was talking to Peter. He had asked me to phone him. I just wanted to see how he was doing, that's all."

"Pati, after all he's put you through, why do you have anything to do with him?"

"I dunno, Mother. He has a way of charming me back into a relationship. But he's considering going on medication. If he does, I think we might have a chance."

Mother would have none of this. "Pati, he's a Dr. Jekyll and Mr. Hyde. One minute he's nice and the next minute he's just plain mean. Can't you see that?"

"I can," I replied. "His moods change rapidly because he's bi-polar, but with meds he could be stabilized."

"I hate to see you wasting so much of your life with this man. I really don't think he's ever going to change. Don't you..."

I stopped her closing argument in its tracks: "It's almost time to leave for the doctor, Mother."

Tonight, as I turn out the living room lights and head for bed, I dismiss the comments Mother made about Peter at breakfast, rationalizing that I have, in fact, made changes in my relationships with men. I divorced Lenny, even if it took me twenty years to do it. That's proof I've grown. So has Lenny, for that matter. He long ago quit drinking, and he was never violent. Neither of us ever hit our sons, who have grown up to be wonderful young men.

In my heart of hearts, however, I know I'm kidding myself about one thing: for four years I've been stuck in an on-again, off-again relationship with a recovering alcoholic who is also bipolar! Shakespeare wrote, "Lovers and madmen have such seething brains." And so do the women who love them.

IV

A Dark Secret Revealed

Gary phones one day in early spring asking me to join him in Harrisburg the coming weekend. It's his turn to be with Mother, but because Joan can't make it, he's hoping I'm free to come and keep him company. I envy my brothers having spouses along when they visit Mother. I have to put up with her all by myself. Even so, Gary and I are close, so I'm happy for the chance to see him for a couple of days.

When I arrive, I find my mother and brother sitting opposite each other in her sitting room. Both look somewhat anxious. Mother doesn't have time for a greeting. She wants to get to her agenda right away. Her first words to me are: "What took you so long? We've been waiting for you. Don't just stand there. Have a seat."

I feel like saying, "Gee, Mom, glad to see you, too." Instead, I drop my canvas overnight bag beside the leather sofa where Gary sits ramrod straight at attention. I take a seat next to him. Mother adjusts her Bentwood rocker to face Gary and me, and gives us each a studied glance before pulling a piece of paper from the pocket of her wrap-around skirt: "This", she announces, "is a copy of the letter I sent to Ken Rowen."

"What's going on, Mother?"

"Pati, don't ask questions! Just listen."

Now we're in familiar drama queen territory. Mother has an annoying habit of refusing to supply background information on the topic at hand. I find this maddeningly controlling. Gary shoots me a rolled-eyeball glance. Mother begins to read:

Dear Ken,

I'm writing to inform you that I can no longer be your patient. The dates and times for appointments and the time it takes to get there are impossible for me. I find it very stressful, which consumes my lessening strength. I will be seeing Dr. Wilson, Rita's new doctor, who is treating her pulmonary fibrosis. I will contact Tracey to have her send my records to Dr. Wilson.

I hope you are enjoying your semi-retirement and all its enrichments.

Best always,
Jane

I'm shocked. Mother's done it! She's actually fired her longtime doctor. Gary is elated, "That's great Mom. You did the right thing, but what brought all this on?"

Jane matter-of-factly replies, "My friend Rita Cohen was seeing a pulmonary specialist at Johns Hopkins but wasn't happy with him. Then someone told her about Dr. Wilson. He specializes in lung diseases. Rita raves about him, and has been trying to convince me to see him too. As Pati knows, Ken keeps me waiting forever. Carla and I waited an hour and a half last week before he saw me."

Mother solicits my opinion, though it's only a formality, "What do you think, Pati?"

"I think it's fabulous. I've always thought Rowen was a pain in the ass. I can never forgive him for the lousy care he gave Dad."

Gary leans in towards me and whispers, "Rowen phoned me two days ago, wanting me to convince Mother to stay with him."

Jane, switching to Miss Marple mode, jumps in, "What's that, Gary? Did you say Ken tried to use you to get me to reconsider? He's got his nerve, going behind my back!"

The doctor she may or may not have had an affair with thirty years before would pay for his indifferent—not to mention incompetent—medical care. Like Gary, I am proud of Mother. Widowhood has given her confidence. Liberated from Dad's domination of every decision, big or small, she's come into her own since his death.

The next day Gary and I take a mid-afternoon coffee break at the mall, where we've been running errands for Mother. I work up the nerve to tell him something I have dreaded, yet longed, to share. It is a secret I have borne alone for too long. I look straight at Gary, and don't mince my words, though I try to speak softly, without emotion: "Gary, there is something I need to tell you. Our grandfather sexually abused Mother. She unburdened herself to me two years ago when we had dinner on my birthday."

Gary stares at the table. I go on: "I don't know if you're aware that Gramps also molested one of our cousins. She told me about it herself several years ago. Gary raises his head and looks at me without saying a word. He protects himself with his unflinching lawyer's façade. As an attorney, Gary is not a stranger to tales of human depravity, but that doesn't prepare him for hearing what happened to his own mother, at the hands of her own father.

I feel compelled to finish the story, despite my brother's obvious reluctance to hear it: "You know the way Mother is only able to let her hair down after she's had a drink or two? Well, halfway through her second Martini that night at supper, Mother suddenly opened up. She looked at me and said, 'Pati, your grandfather did things to me he never should have.' She didn't use the words 'sexual abuse'—she didn't have to—but she did say that it went on for a long time. I started to cry, but Mother seemed so tough, so stoic that I couldn't allow myself to break down, so I used all my strength to hold back tears. After that I felt an incredible rage against Gramps. I wanted him to come back from the grave so I could punch him in the face and scream at him! As soon as I returned home I took all the photos of him and Nana out of their frames and cut him out of the pictures. To think that Mother carried this terrible secret and terrible shame alone for so many years."

My brother rises from his chair without a word and goes to the counter for a refill. He returns to the table and sits down. Finally he speaks: "This is pretty awful stuff." After a long pause, he adds, "I guess we should get back to our shopping."

V

A Figment of My Dysfunction

Returning home from the public radio station in Syracuse, where I host a weekly show called Women's Voices, I decide to indulge in my favorite outdoor therapy: gardening. It's a perfect June evening, comfortably warm and with enough daylight left to be outside for an hour or two. After blissfully troweling in the dark, moist earth for a while, I hear the phone ringing through my open kitchen window. I wipe my muddy fingers on my shorts and dash inside to pick up the receiver. It's my brother Nate, explaining that he and Gary are both tied up the coming weekend. Upshot: it's up to me to go to Harrisburg to be with Mother. A family member should be present when Hospice visits her for the first time.

We've known for a couple of weeks that it's time, and mother has accepted the idea of having visits from Hospice workers, though she still resists the idea of overnight help. The reality of Hospice entering the picture cuts me to the quick: *Omigod, Mother really is dying!*

During the four-hour drive to Harrisburg I begin to dwell on my chronic anger toward Mother, picturing myself in women's circles for the rest of my life. These support groups are just like the late-night college bull sessions where my friends and I used to recycle our gripes and come to the same conclusion: our mothers were to blame for the way our lives turned out.

Each of the women in my close circle of graduate school friends had her own "mother story." Jill's mother had failed her because she drank too much. Ruth's mother because she made her husband more important than her children. Linda's mother, like mine, was too narcissistic to be present for her daughter. Lisa's mother was so cowed by her husband that she never once defended her daughter against her father's unfair criticisms.

In our private moments my friends and I knew we were not being completely fair. Every child tends to enlarge a mother's missteps and excuse her own. But when my group got together we were riding a runaway train: once we hit the tracks of mother-blame, there was no stopping us.

In the late 1960s when I was studying for my master's degree in social work, my classmates and I pored over the literature of child rearing. Practically all of it over-blamed mothers for their children's outcomes. It would be twenty years before family therapy would assimilate the pioneering research on women done in the 1970s and 1980s. Although Simone de Beauvoir had written The Second Sex back in 1949 and Betty Friedan published The Feminine Mystique in 1963, there was nothing comparable in the academic literature until 1976, when Jean Baker Miller published her seminal work, Toward a New Psychology of Women.

Miller's book led to the founding of the Stone Center at Wellesley College, where she was a professor, and to a whole new therapeutic framework for diagnosing and treating women and families. Noted women psychologists and psychiatrists came together at the Stone Center to formulate new theories of feminine development that explained how girls and women are adversely molded and judged by the prevailing culture.

Meanwhile, at Harvard, Dr. Carol Gilligan produced compelling data showing that the average girl was just as independent as the average boy when young, but when girls reached their teens they, unlike boys, tended to lose that independence.

From 1982 to 1997 I was part of a support group made up of women therapists, who met for peer supervision. At one of those meetings during the Eighties a member excitedly opened up her brief case to produce a thin paper document with a blue cover, entitled, "Work in Progress from the Stone Center." This particular paper described how women are relational creatures: they tend to forge their identities in groups of other women. This was a direct challenge to traditional psychology with its emphasis on separation as the key to individuality. My colleagues and I instantly recognized ourselves in the report and knew that the Stone Center was breaking new ground. We often read Stone Center papers before they found their way into books.

These papers changed my life, forcing me to rethink almost everything I had been taught in graduate school. Over time I learned to trust my instincts, to champion empathy and to question the prevailing cultural model of seeking personal empowerment rather than shared leadership within a community.

One year, while I was involved with The Women's Project in Family Therapy, I invited Mother to accompany me to Boston for a mother-daughter conference. Jane thoroughly enjoyed herself, but in one large-group session, when I leaned over and whispered something to her that had popped into my head, she immediately raised her hand and declared, "My daughter has a question for you." The audience of therapists roared. Jane seemed surprised.

Later, when I made a report to my women's group about the Boston weekend, a typical reaction was "Wow! Your mother joined you. My mother would never do that."

Jane did it again the next year, this time in Wellfleet on Cape Cod. As before, all of the participants were therapists accompanied by their mothers. Jane and I volunteered for one of the role-playing sessions. In her usual way, Mother talked on and on about herself. I will always remember the facilitator looking at her and saying, "Jane, you do not listen to Patricia." Mother told me later "I *always* listen to you."

Nevertheless, the Women's Project left its mark on Jane. My brother Gary was in Harrisburg when Mother returned from Wellfleet. He phoned me in amazement to say, "Mom is challenging Dad like crazy, telling him again and again that he is sexist!" (When people ask me why my brothers call Jane "Mom" and I call her "Mother," I explain that when I was around twelve, she began to insist that I call her Mother because it sounded more dignified.)

I arrive at Mother's apartment at 12:30, just half an hour before the appointment with the Hospice nurse. Mother is in the kitchen trying to decide what to "serve the guest." I remind her that this is not an afternoon tea; it's a meeting with a professional, a chance for her to learn more about Hospice and establish a rapport.

My remarks trigger Mother's defenses and provoke her to challenge me: "Why do I need to have rapport with Hospice? I know that I have a terminal illness, and I don't need people hovering around me."

I resist a retort, reverting to my well-rehearsed role as lady-in-waiting. I go to the kitchen and prepare a tray of iced tea and chocolate chip cookies for "the guest."

Right on time, at exactly one o'clock, the doorbell rings. I answer it and greet a middle-aged, solidly built woman with short curly hair and a confident smile. She introduces herself as "Lee" and continues talking as she approaches Mother. Lee plants herself in front of Jane and shakes mother's hand vigorously; then she plops down on the sofa, her ample bottom provoking a small squawk from the leather pillow. Lee's take-charge demeanor makes me smile inside. I wonder how Mother will manage her.

After only twenty minutes it's apparent that Lee has made it to the winner's circle. She has disarmed Mother by praising her delicious cookies and her gorgeous furnishings. Lee even includes me in her charm campaign, as she compliments a "good-looking mother and daughter." She shows Mother photos of her own children.

Once she's warmed Mother up, Lee asks Jane how she's been feeling. To my surprise Mother makes a candid report. She readily describes her diminished appetite and admits that she has upped her oxygen intake. Lee suggests that she take Megace, an appetite stimulant, which is often used by Aids patients. Mother likes the idea of joining ranks with Aids patients. She tells Lee, "I had so many nice gay men as customers when I had my antique shop. I think a few of them had Aids."

The Seventies was my vintage clothing decade. I hunted down lawn sales and haunted consignment shops and antique stores to find unique outfits, preferring the swanky, shoulder-padded fashions of the 1940s. My ex-husband used to remark that I smelled of mothballs. Adam, at age seven, precociously commented, "You look like that lady who was mean to her children." (He had seen the trailer for Mommy Dearest on television.)

At least my *retro* wardrobe was glamorous. I can't say the same for my "vampire" period during college, when I favored all-black garb and gauntly pale makeup. Dad once quipped, "Maybe I can get you a job with my friend Tom Allen after you graduate." Tom Allen ran a funeral home.

One of Mother's endearing traits is her thoughtfulness. Whenever she learns about a special interest you have, she does all she can to accommodate it. Happily for me, my vintage period coincided with the time when

Mother owned the antique store. One summer evening she phoned me with the announcement, "On your next trip to Harrisburg, we will have to visit *Andrew*." Andrew was one of Mother's favorite gay customers. "He's small, like you, Pati, and he's getting rid of his current wardrobe."

When we eventually visited him in his big, funky apartment, Andrew greeted us warmly and then whisked me into his bedroom and opened the door to his huge closet. It was shoulder-pad heaven!

I tried on one outfit after another, dashing from the bedroom to the living room to model them for my audience of two. Mother and Andrew responded with thumbs up or thumbs down as they sat on his sagging sofa drinking beer from bottles. My acquisitions that day were to die-for: a black bear fur jacket, beaded sweaters, a Pendleton plaid shirt, some glamorous V-neck dresses and even a satin nightgown a la Carole Lombard. Mother seemed as delighted as I was with my haul.

Remembering this incident now, I'm reminded of what my sister-in-law Joan once said to me, "You're lucky to have a mother who's so much fun."

By the end of Lee's visit Mother has agreed to see her weekly, and gives a tentative OK to a visit from a Hospice social worker, but she turns down the offer to have a Hospice minister stop by. Despite all that has happened to rob her of it, Mother has not lost her independence.

On Sunday, as I set off for Syracuse, I find myself wondering why my friends and I, despite all that we now know about feminine psychology and family dynamics, still tend to blame our mothers and let our fathers off the hook. A novel thought takes me by surprise: what if "The Woman Who Ruined My Life" is only a figment of my own dysfunctional imagination -- the mother of my invention?

VI

A Motherless Child?

My brothers and I have always taken to heart our parents' example of serving the community. Gary, who has been a lawyer in Milwaukee for twenty-five years, routinely adjusts his fees to what his clients can pay. His victories against police brutality and sexual harassment have sometimes made the front-page news of the Milwaukee newspapers. Nate, who is an architect, channels his skills into volunteer work with Habitat for Humanity. He and his wife Rose have also participated in Mideast peace and reconciliation projects sponsored by their upstate New York Quaker community.

Ever since my college days, when I was transformed by reading Simone de Beauvoir's The Second Sex, working for women's equality has been central to my life. I've belonged to numerous activist groups, written letters to the editor on a regular basis, and lost count of the number of marches and demonstrations I've been part of over the years.

I've paid a price for my views, however. In the mid-1990s -- some twenty years after the heyday of the Women's Movement, and after a successful eight-year run writing a popular advice column called Coping -- a new editor at the paper fired me.

The explanation? "Your column is too controversial." What I think she meant was that my column was too feminist. My loyal readers swamped the newspaper with letters and phone calls, insisting that I be reinstated, but the paper wouldn't budge.

Just when I thought I would never work in that town again, a friend at the local NPR affiliate rescued me. He offered me the chance to produce short segments featuring women of distinction. This opportunity led me to create and host a new weekly radio program, Women's Voices, which debuted in 1998. The show won a Clarion Award for Best Women's Issues Radio in 2000 and 2002.

My mother was fascinated by my accounts of marching in support of Roe v. Wade in Washington DC and at the state Capitol. Mother had always believed in women's reproductive rights, but had kept her views largely to herself. I think my own activism empowered her, because eventually she began to speak her mind when confronted with opposing views at various Republican social events she and Dad attended. Mother would often phone me to report that she had taken a political stand. She seemed to be seeking my approval. I was quick to support her and was especially proud of her when she was asked to be on the board of the Harrisburg chapter of Planned Parenthood.

Despite the fact that I had championed a woman's right to choose, I never thought that I would ever need to consider having an abortion myself. Then, following a New Year's Eve party in the late Seventies, I forgot to use my diaphragm when my husband and I made love. Six weeks later I learned that I was pregnant.

I was flabbergasted because I didn't remember failing to use protection that night. I had always thought that women who got pregnant when they didn't intend to were simply irresponsible. Now I realized how easy it was to slip up. I was equally surprised at how ambivalent I felt about exercising my right to choose.

My decision to have an abortion was a wrenching one. After some agonizing, sleepless nights and countless discussions with Lenny (whose standard response was always, "Do what you think is best.") I came to the conclusion that a third child would be more than I could manage. Our two sons were still pre-school age, and I had recently begun a demanding new job as Director of Counseling at a local college. Jobs were hard to come by in our small community, and we needed the income. I didn't see how I could do justice to a newborn baby as well as my two small children and my job.

So much shame was attached to having an abortion that I kept mine a secret, even from my closest friends. On the afternoon when "the procedure" was scheduled, I informed the Dean of Students that I didn't feel well, and would be going home. Lenny drove me to the hospital. This was the same hospital where I had worked the year before as a social worker. The Ob-Gyn nurses knew me. While they had once been friendly, on this day they were curt. The nurse who escorted me to the examining room looked me in the eyes, shook her head, and said, "You, of all people."

After the abortion was over I was exhausted, shaken and disoriented. As I began to exit the Ob-Gyn unit, the nurse at the desk called out to me: "Not so fast. There's one more thing you have to do." Like a high school principal about to discipline a student, she thrust a piece of paper toward me: "You have to sign the death certificate."

In my wildest dreams, I would never have imagined that such a requirement was possible. A *baby* had not died. It wasn't even a fetus. It was still an embryo. Do they require death certificates for the embryos routinely destroyed by fertility clinics? Stunned, humiliated and too weak to resist, I rapidly scribbled my signature where the nurse pointed, silently vowing never to return to this hospital.

Lenny met me downstairs and suggested we have lunch in the hospital cafeteria before going home. Staying there for lunch was the last thing I wanted to do, but I was still too dazed and distressed to say so. While Lenny chatted jovially with an intern he knew at the next table I stared at my tuna fish sandwich, feeling miserable. I'm sure he was happy to have the distraction from the reason we were there, but it left me feeling so alone, just as I had been in making my decision. I wanted Lenny to take my hand and comfort me, but I felt too unworthy to ask for this.

The shock of being told I must sign a death certificate intensified my post-abortion guilt. For months afterward, particularly whenever I ran into a friend with a baby, I felt like a murderer.

On the drive home from the hospital Lenny and I sat in silence, wrapped in our separate cocoons, barely able to look at each other, let alone talk. I could not bring myself to speak of the horrible thing I had done for a long time. Instead I would slip away to the basement, where Lenny and the boys could not hear me cry. It was the worst place I could have chosen because even in the dark I could see the crib that Sam and Adam had slept in as infants. I saw in it the ghost of the child I had given up. And I mourned that child alone. Perhaps Lenny was mourning, too, but like me, he avoided mentioning the abortion for decades afterward.

I believe to this day that my abortion irretrievably altered our marriage, creating a gulf between us that could not be filled, though Lenny attempted to fill it with affairs. Many years after we were divorced and had left the acrimony of that difficult time behind us, Lenny stunned me by saying "You know, I often think of the daughter we might have had." If Lenny had wanted me to go on with my pregnancy in hopes that we might have a girl, why hadn't he said so when I begged him to help me make the decision? Or was this just a case of sentimental thinking after the fact? I kept my reactions to myself. Years of separation dull the appetite for argument.

Two months after the abortion I decided to tell Mother what I'd done. She and Dad were visiting us in Oneonta for the weekend. When Mother and I got in the car to go home after browsing through antique stores in nearby Cooperstown, I blurted out the news.

Mother's first words in response were, "I won't tell your father." As I started the car, I glanced at Mother and nodded appreciatively. My somber revelation left us enveloped in silence for a few minutes, until my feelings became too strong to be contained. Sobbing quietly I confessed to an over-powering sense of guilt.

In a rare moment in my adult life, Mother touched me. She reached across the space between our seats and stroked my arm, offering me words of comfort, "Don't talk like that, Pati. You did what you had to." Then she placed her hand on my shoulder and said, "Now let it go and get on with your life. You have two wonderful sons. You're a good mother to Adam and Sam."

A few months later I wrote a letter to the editor of the New York Times in response to an op-ed piece written by a well-known reporter, Lynda Bird Franke, who described her anguish over her own abortion. Franke's ambivalence and pain resonated with me. The New York Times printed my letter, which I signed "Anonymous" for fear of repercussions at my job if I used my name. Mother astonished me by phoning the day my letter appeared. It was dinnertime and I was busy in the kitchen.

"Pati, are you alone?" Mother addressed me in an impatient whisper.

"Yes, I'm alone except for the boys, who are watching TV. Is anything wrong?"

"Nothing's wrong. I called because I saw your letter in today's New York Times. I could tell it was from you even though you didn't sign your name."

I was dumbfounded.

Now I find myself wondering what happened to that wise, caring mother? Where did she go? Am I too blocked, too angry to acknowledge her?

In the produce section of Wegmans I run into Hilda, a good friend who is also a therapist. She affectionately tells me that I look terrible. I tell her I'm wracked with guilt because despite the fact that my mother is dying, most of the time I don't feel the least upset about it. Hilda fishes in her purse for a pen and paper and writes down the number of a minister who counsels relatives of dying patients.

Back at home I put away my groceries and place the call, feeling that if I don't phone right away, I never will. The minister recognizes my name from my newspaper column and radio show. We agree on a day to meet.

At the appointed time I knock on his door and am greeted by a graying, middle-aged man of medium height and build, dressed in a dark charcoal suit with a clerical collar. He offers an encouraging smile and tells me to call him "Reverend Dave."

When he asks why I'm here, I reply urgently, "My Mother is dying and I don't feel sad. I want to feel more, but I can't. We never had a very affectionate relationship."

Rev. Dave means well, but his canned advice leaves me cold: "Try telling your mother how much she means to you." *Disingenuous.* "Take an interest in her daily routines." *Simplistic.* "Why not make a photo scrapbook of your mother to remember her by?" *Not another scrapbook!* Despite all of this, I schedule an appointment for the following week.

I arrive home from my session with Rev. Dave to find a message on my phone machine from my brother Nate, who wants me to call him back. As I dial Nate's number my heart beats rapidly. Mother is visiting Nate and Rose. Nate doesn't usually phone unless there's a problem. He answers the phone cheerfully. They're having cocktails before supper now, he explains, but earlier in the day Mother had another mishap. She was alone in the house and fell. When Nate and Rose got home, they found her sitting quietly on the porch, looking frightened. When pressed, Mother explained her fall by saying she felt dizzy when she got up from her chair too quickly. She spoke rapidly in between short breaths, leading Nate to speculate that she was experiencing a mild anxiety attack. As a precaution, Rose phoned the nearby Hospice, which sent a nurse over right away. Mother confessed to the nurse that she hadn't been using her oxygen. That alone might have caused her dizzy spell and subsequent fall.

Because of this episode, Nate suggests that he and I and Gary schedule a conference call for next week to discuss getting overnight help for Mother. "I'm fully aware that the topic is a minefield," Nate sighs, "but I don't think we have a choice. Mom can no longer be alone at night."

Heaven help me! It's my weekend to visit Mother, which means that I've drawn the short straw. It will be up to me to persuade her to accept the extra help. Nate and Gary echo each other's reassurances:

"You have a way with Mother."

"She'll listen to you."

I feel like I've been conned. When has Mother ever yielded to me or anyone else in the family?

By Sunday afternoon my time is running out. I enter Mother's bedroom where she's "resting" on the bed. Mother never "naps." I cautiously state that Nate, Gary and I are concerned for her safety, given the growing number of her falls. Before she can snap back I add quickly, "Gary and Nate and I would like to foot the bill for a nurse's aide at night so that someone's here in case you fall and can't phone for help."

Mother is incensed at this suggestion. She snaps, "I'm not going to have a stranger in my home!"

I plead, "Try to put yourself in our shoes, Mother. We worry about you. We would feel at fault if something bad happened to you."

This makes Mother even madder. She repeats her position so loudly that I fear the people in the next apartment can hear her, "For the last time, Pati, I am not having a stranger in my home!"

I back off. I can at least report to my brothers that I gave it my best try.

Ten minutes later I'm packing up when I hear a thud in the direction of Mother's room. I race to the bedroom and find her on the floor with her back against the bed, struggling to get up. I help her stand and guide her into her La-Z-Boy. Then I lose it: "This is absurd. Look what just happened, Mother! Clearly you do need someone around. You're falling all the time now."

Mother glares back at me, resembling a comic book character whose irises have been replaced by lightning bolts. She lashes out, "Pati, I've always had dizzy spells. This is nothing new. Don't you start in on me!"

I snap back, "Mother, it's time you faced reality. You're sick. Your body is not what it was. Sooner or later you're going to have to accept help. I think the time is now."

Mother sputters anxiously. Her breath is short and she punctuates her phrases with deep, dramatic gasps: "Pati! You're upsetting me. Stop this right now!"

I panic. I don't want her to have an anxiety attack. I apologize over and over. Mother seizes her advantage. Clenching the arms of her La-Z-Boy, she spits out her ultimatum, "The *subject* -- of night-time *help* -- is *closed*."

Mother morphs into her Ice Queen persona for the remainder of my stay, barely talking to me, focusing her attention on the Sunday newspapers and writing notes to friends. When it's time for me to leave, she is chatting on the phone and doesn't interrupt her conversation, even to say "Goodbye." She simply waves me out the door.

I am smoking mad as I throw my bag in the car and stab the key into the ignition. I drive away in tears, heading into the embrace of a roiling black sky. A summer thunderstorm is on the way. I feel profoundly unloved and alone, as if I am already an orphan.

VII

Stumbling Toward Intimacy

I'm awash in advice. My massage therapist, who happens to be a former Hospice nurse, encourages me to play some tapes from my radio show for Mother as a way to connect with her. Rev. Dave tells me to mourn my "failed mother-daughter relationship." A staffer on Women's Voices suggests a last ditch solution: "Mother *yourself*."

By the time I'm off to spend the weekend in Harrisburg, my confusion has intensified: What can I say that won't set Mother off? How should I respond when she becomes hyper-controlling? How can I get myself to relax around her?

For the moment, I'll have to settle for a peace offering. I stop on the outskirts of Harrisburg to purchase a bouquet of Stargazer lilies, one of her favorite flowers.

As I enter Mother's apartment I hear an unfamiliar male voice coming from her bedroom. It sounds young. Mother is laughing, maybe even flirting. I call out, "Hello. It's me, Pati."

Mother's voice is filled with animation, "Pati, come in here and meet Ron, my new

Hospice nurse." Well, this is a pleasant change. Mother's ambivalence towards Hospice has been replaced by giddy acceptance. Ron is an extremely handsome young man in his late twenties, at most. I'm confident that Mother will look forward to his visits. Ron cordially shakes my hand while he explains that he'll be sharing Mother's care with Lee.

Today, Ron will instruct Mother in the use of a medical device: a nebulizer. The squat green metal machine is the size of a vacuum canister and is presently ensconced in a corner of her bedroom. She will be using the nebulizer three times a day, breathing through a mouthpiece to receive additional oxygen. Mother shoos me away, telling me it's time for her lesson and reminding me to cut the stems of the flowers before putting them in water. I exit her room as she continues her light-hearted banter with Ron. Her mood is at odds with what the nebulizer represents: the progression of her illness.

While waiting for Mother and Ron to finish, I step out onto her long balcony. Last summer the window boxes on the balcony wall were spilling over with cascading white petunias and trailing ivy; the lion-faced urns near the living room door showcased red geraniums. Now everything is empty. The black wrought iron chairs look somber without their floral seat cushions.

Ron invites me back to Mother's room to retrieve her pill bottles so that he can write down the dosages. I gather up her medication and take it into the kitchen. For the first time it strikes me how many different pills she takes every day: morphine for the back pain, pills to maintain a regular heartbeat, pills to help with urination, a nasal spray, pills to bring on sleep, and a variety of vitamins. It suddenly hits me how much energy and focus dying requires. Dying is a full time job.

At some point after Mother's death, on a trip to Harrisburg to visit Aunt Gerda, I would run into Ron and learn that Mother had been one of his favorite patients. She'd given him a photo of herself that he still kept on his dresser.

After Ron leaves, I decide to take advantage of Mother's positive frame of mind to broach the *D* word. I don't know why but for the past few weeks I've been obsessed by the desire to know how Mother feels about dying. Maybe the therapist in me thinks it will help to crack her denial. Maybe I'm hoping it will help me when it's my turn to die. Logical Pati warns me that asking Mother a question like this might be dangerous, but Emotional Pati is in the driver's seat. I steel myself and plunge right in: "Mother, I was wondering if you ever think about dying."

Mother throws me a look that says, *Well, you have your nerve.* She delivers a curt answer, "I run out of oxygen. I die. They come and take me away in a body bag. I'm cremated, and that's it."

I'm too stunned to know what to say, but, like an idiot, I proceed anyway, "You know, Mother, I share the Hindu belief in reincarnation. I believe that although our physical bodies die, our souls endure. They cast about for a while but eventually they inhabit a new physical form. I find this comforting."

Mother all but sneers, "Oh, so I can look forward to coming back as a bird or a cat?" I set myself up for that one.

Jane signals she's through with this conversation by picking up the new issue of TIME and flipping through its pages. I leave and go to the kitchen to make a cup of tea and collect myself. As I stare at the steam kettle, Carla's remark at Christmas time comes back to me: "Your mother is very fragile, Pati." She doesn't seem so fragile at times like this, but I realize that I'm starting to see a pattern. Aside from the fact that she is simply not religious, Mother's heads-on responses are her armor against intimacy. She's not the stoic she pretends to be.

Later that same day, after I return from a stroll along the riverfront, Mother calls to me from her bedroom, "Come here, Pati. I've been thinking."

Wondering what's to come, I enter her room and approach the La-Z-Boy, where she spends more and more of her time now. I pull up a chair beside her, full of curiosity.

Mother's voice sounds small and helpless. "You must think I'm awful because I don't want to talk about dying, or what happens to me after I die."

Her honesty is disarming. I look at Mother with tears in my eyes. I want to cry and embrace her, but I fear it's chancing too much. Instead, I try to reassure her, "No, Mother, I don't judge you. I just wondered how you felt."

In a soft voice, Mother replies, "I just don't think about death, Pati. I know I have a terminal illness. I hope I can make it through the holidays, that's all."

VIII

Secret Depository

With Hillary Clinton's Senate run in full swing, I've been dogging her staff for months in pursuit of an interview. Finally, towards the end of August, I get a call saying Mrs. Clinton has had a cancellation and can do a phone interview today, just two hours from now. I'm a bundle of nerves as I drive to the station, where Lucy, my producer, meets me. We reserve a studio and quickly make a list of questions. When the time comes to speak to Hillary, my jitters disappear and I end up with twenty minutes of tape. Outside the studio, Lucy and I whoop and holler like schoolgirls at our triumph: we're the first media outlet in Central New York to land an in-depth interview with the candidate.

I decide to take my massage therapist's advice and play this tape for Mother. Jane listens attentively, not taking her eyes off the tape recorder until it clicks off. Mother praises my skills and muses, "I wonder why Hillary put up with Bill's womanizing all those years."

I resist reminding Jane that she put up with Richard's dalliances for far longer. Her own infidelities -- one affair that I'm sure of and another that may or may not have occurred -- had more to do with revenge than promiscuity.

My mind flashes back to when I was a teenager and Mother first began to keep me abreast of the extra-marital adventures of Richard The Two-Timer. I remember one summer evening in particular, when I was sixteen and we were all seated around the dining room table for dinner. Just as Mother was about to serve the food, Dad bolted from his chair, explaining that he had to dash to the office to pick up some papers he forgot. Mother beckoned me to the kitchen on the pretext that she needed help. Standing beside me at the counter, she whispered, "Your father forgot to return a motel key. I saw it on his dresser. That's why he left just now, to take it back."

As an adult I came to realize that it was unfair (to say the least) for Mother to make me her secret depository. It was not the kind of intimacy I craved. Years later, as a social worker, I would still find it tough to admit that "dysfunctional" was a label that fit our affluent family as aptly as it did the families of my welfare clients.

There was one secret that Mother kept even from me. I discovered it by accident after I was married. Lenny and I and eighteen-month old Sam were on a road trip to Washington, DC. On the spur of the moment we decided to stop off in Harrisburg to say hello to my family. Instead of Mother, it was Nana who answered the door, explaining that Jane was in the hospital. She added, "It's not serious. Your mother doesn't want any visitors."

Ignoring Nana's objections I left Lenny and Sam at the house and drove straight to the hospital. My unexpected appearance startled Mother, who was propped up in bed staring out the window, in a room devoid of the customary get-well cards and flowers. Mother smiled weakly at me.

I urgently inquired, "Why are you here?"

Before answering, Mother glanced nervously around the room and took a few sips of water from the glass on her night table. "Do you really want to know?"

"Absolutely. That's why I'm here."

"Promise me you won't tell anyone."

"I promise. Please, Mother, what's happened?"

"Your father gave me a sexually transmitted disease. The infection is pretty bad. Dr. Warner admitted me to the hospital for a few days so they could load me up with antibiotics and keep an eye on me."

"Oh Mother, I'm so sorry. Where *is* Dad, anyway? Shouldn't he be around for moral support?"

"He's out of town on business."

I've never been angrier at my father than I was at that moment. I pleaded with Mother to divorce him: "You can make a better life for yourself. Never forget that you are a beautiful, charming, accomplished woman." Not only did Jane run her own business but she was highly regarded in the community for her civic involvement.

Mother studied my face carefully, and nodded, acknowledging the validity of my argument; but as much as she might have longed to be free of my father, she just couldn't imagine her life apart from Dad. She sighed, "I could never leave your father because of the family. He likes having you and Gary and Nate and the grandchildren visit. How would he manage all by himself?"

What Mother really meant was that family, or her version of it, meant everything to *her*. It has taken me all these years to realize that Mother was determined not to let anything mar her ideal image of our perfect, and perfectly accomplished, family.

As the eldest child, my mission was to protect this image at all costs. I also came to understand why I, unlike my brothers, was sent away to summer camp, starting at age ten; and why I was packed off to boarding school at age fifteen. I had failed my charge in some ways. While I kept Mother's secrets, I was also the family "truth teller," threatening the viability of the family myth by complaining to Mother about the tension in the household, or arguing with Dad about his unfairness to us kids. Sending me away insured a calmer household because my younger brothers seldom challenged our parents. Perhaps that was why they were never sent off to camp or boarding school. One summer, as Mother was helping me pack for camp, I decided to ask her about that.

She replied, "I couldn't send your brothers to camp--I'd miss them too much." As young as I was at the time, I knew she didn't mean to hurt me with this comment. She was simply oblivious to what her answer implied.

IX

Command Appearance

Mother has invited the whole family to Harrisburg for Labor Day weekend. My brothers and I inform our children that this is a command appearance, emphasizing that it could be the last time we are all together because Mom-Mom's health is rapidly declining. She spends her days in the La-Z-Boy because she no longer has the stamina to walk. Some days she still manages to get dressed, but most of the time she is in her bedclothes and bathrobe.

Mother has one guest room, which I have been occupying at her request. The rest of the family book rooms across the street at the Marriott, just as they did last Christmas. By late Saturday morning the clan has gathered in the apartment.

In small groups we take turns going into Mother's bedroom for short visits. The conversation is focused on everyone's future plans, as if to reassure Mother we'll all be fine after she's gone. Nate and Rose bring up a future trip to Israel while Gary and Joan describe a planned addition to their home. Sam and Mary discuss their marriage plans. My stomach turns over at the thought that Mother won't be there for my son's wedding, or for any other family events in the future.

Mother herself avoids talking about the future; she focuses instead on happy times from the past. I'm grateful for her positive memories because they help to assuage a guilty feeling I cannot shake, that somehow I've been a bad daughter. She reminisces fondly about the summers when she sat in on the Women's Spirituality classes I taught at the Chautauqua Institution.

Her first time in my class occurred just a few months after Dad died. Privately I had told the women in the class about Mother's new widowed state. The group made an effort to draw her out, lingering after the class to talk to her or to invite her to lunch.

By the second year she came to my class Mother felt comfortable enough to interrupt me in mid-sentence to point out that I had overlooked a woman who had her hand raised. She would audibly gasp when my politics were too radical for her, but that didn't diminish her enthusiasm for the experience. When we were alone she praised my teaching and told me how much she enjoyed her classmates. We might laugh about an unexpectedly funny incident, or exchange an affectionate smile over something tender, like the young mother who brought her infant child along to every class.

Why haven't we been able to recapture the wonderful closeness we experienced during those Chautauqua summers?

On Saturday evening Nate surprises us by saying that we're going to have a champagne toast. The thirteen of us crowd into Mother's room. A few among the older generation flank her Laz-Z-Boy; some of the grandchildren sit cross-legged on the floor while others perch on the fancy wicker folding chairs Mother originally purchased to accommodate large dinner parties. There is a sudden lull in the room, as if the significance of what we are about to do has dawned on everyone at the same moment. We glance nervously at each other, hoping that someone will break the ice. Leave it to Mother to take care of that. She surveys the room, then smiles before eliciting one of her signature girlish laughs: "I don't know when I've seen so many people in my bedroom."

Adam and Stephen pass around the goblets of champagne. When everyone has a glass, Nate raises his and declares, "Here's to Mother. To her love of family."

Mother smiles appreciatively, "Thank you, Nate. I couldn't ask for a nicer family."

I struggle to hold back my tears, exchanging sad smiles with Joan, who is also welling up. In short order we drain three bottles of Mother's favorite bubbly, Korbel.

Mother manages a few sips and becomes very quiet. We take our cue and leave her room to help with dinner.

Just as we're about to sit down at the table, the doorbell rings, but we're not expecting anyone. To our surprise and annoyance, it's Gordon, Mother's sometime boyfriend who is now in the grip of dementia. He storms into Mother's room. In a loud voice he barks at her, "What are you doing in a bathrobe? Get up! We have a date to go dancing tonight."

Mother adopts the calm voice she perfected over the years of living with Dad's angry outbursts. "I can't go dancing tonight, Gordon. As you can see, the whole family is here and we're about to have dinner."

Gordon is undeterred. He moves within inches of Mother, and shouts, "Jane, this is our night to go dancing. Now get ready!"

Again Mother tries to reason with Gordon, who grows even more agitated. He slams a hairbrush down on her dresser. Gary and Nate have been watching from the doorway, staying back because Mother has signaled them not to interfere, but this is too much. They spring into action. My brothers take Gordon in hand, each grabbing one of his arms. They hustle him out the apartment door and into an elevator. Downstairs they fold Gordon into a taxi and climb in on either side of him to ensure that he gets home safely.

Joan and I and Nate's wife Rose have remained with Mother in her room. She makes a comment tinged with weary anger, "I'm dying and I'm still taking care of others." The three of us exchange helpless looks, but no one speaks.

X

Thank You, Mae West

After yet another break-up with Peter, who is off his meds again, I decide to celebrate my birthday alone in New York City on the first weekend of October.

Without medication Peter always goes into manic high gear, his ego blazing, his concern for anyone or anything else a casualty of the road. Peter's lack of sympathy for what I am going through in my own life infuriates me, supplying me with the courage to kick him out.

On the plane I resolve to leave my loneliness and self-doubt behind, but once I land I realize that being middle-aged and alone in Manhattan is not the way to do that. New York City can be a cruel environment for the older woman. Everywhere I look, it seems, there is a beautiful young woman relishing the attention she commands from passing strangers. Attractive men my age look away when we pass in the street, while much older men eye me as a prospect.

Friday evening I have dinner with two longtime friends who are single and living alone. Arlene and Jill each confess to a long-

ing for marriage, or at least for a steady relationship with a man. Back in my hotel room,
I think about our dinner conversation, and
realize that my friends' neediness made me
uncomfortable. As much as I would like to be
in a healthy, loving relationship, I don't want
this desire to rule my life. I want to feel ful-
filled as a person in my own right so that
I don't spend my twilight years feeling I'm
incomplete without a man. I say a little
prayer before I turn in, asking for help finding contentment as an older single woman.

Saturday night I see a hilarious play
about Mae West that brings back a fond memory I have of Nana. At her eightieth birthday
party she made a show-stopping entrance as a
Mae West look-alike, wearing a form-fitting
sequined dress that enhanced her ample bust
line. Some of the older guests were taken
aback, but my brothers and I loved our
grandmother's flamboyant sense of fun.

Fashion is my forte. Like Nana, I love
dramatic outfits that signal my arrival at social gatherings.

I have fond memories of Nana taking me
to Pomeroy's Department Store for lunch
when I was a teenager. Afterward we would
head for the jewelry department, trying on as
many necklaces and earrings as we could before the irritated clerk figured out that we
had no intention of purchasing anything.
Then we'd move on to hats and designer

clothing, where we repeated our shameless fun before heading home.

Mother herself had little sense of fashion, but she admired mine, and deferred to my wardrobe suggestions. On one of these occasions I surveyed her closet in search of a party dress, proclaiming, "Everything in here is outdated. We're going shopping right now!" My favorite find for her that day was a peach-tinted chiffon dress with a long attached scarf. I dubbed it "the Gloria Swanson." Mother protested that it was "too much" for her, but when the sales clerk told her how beautiful she looked, she relented.

Unlike Nana and me, Mother was far from flamboyant, even when she was dressed to the nines; but like Mae West, she had perfected the art of flirting. At cocktail parties she was usually surrounded by men. Mother even flirted with my college boyfriends -- to my chagrin -- though I'm confident that she never went as far as Mrs. Robinson in The Graduate.

Nana and Mother and I did have one thing in common: we were all suckers for men who were no good for us.

I think about that as I walk back to my hotel on my birthday night, wishing I could be as feisty and independent as Mae West, who always seemed to be in the driver's seat, on or off the stage.

Back at home on Sunday I go through my accumulated mail. Among my birthday cards is one from Mother. Inside it she has enclosed an uncharacteristically long letter whose shaky penmanship bears only a faint resemblance to Mother's once beautiful floral script:

Dear Pati,

The day you were born was a happy day for Richard and me. Our first-born was so pretty and lively. Through the years it has not always been easy for you, but somehow your struggles gave you an appreciation of life, and the strength to overcome the many rough bumps you have had.

Sam and Adam love you and care about you very much. I'm so happy that you will all be with me for Thanksgiving. Mary's presence will be the icing on the cake.

Don't feel sad about Peter. He couldn't be real with you. He's attractive, intelligent, and witty, but underneath he's very troubled. Don't cry anymore over him. You tried to make him happy with you. He had it all. It's his loss.

You have changed in many ways. I think you are more attractive – you look younger. Your mood is easier and you seem to have more self-control. You have accomplished so much – your newspaper column, the radio show, and all the work you've done in Syracuse on behalf of women. I'm proud of you and all that you've accomplished.

Remember, Pati, you are a strong, self-made woman. You have so much.

I love you,
Mother

At this moment I experience a pure, uncomplicated love for Mother. It's as if someone has vacuumed my brain, sucking out layers and layers of conflicting thoughts and feelings. I am moved to my core. Becalmed, I feel sleep coming on.

The next morning I pour a mug of coffee and reach for my note cards. I select a card with calla lilies, her favorite flower, and take up my pen:

Dear Mother,

Thank you for the loving birthday sentiments. I value deeply your encouraging words. In spite of all my years of therapy, I still put myself down. In New York I saw a play about Mae West who, as you know, had no trouble thinking well of herself. It would serve me well to incorporate some of her chutzpah!

I'm making a vow to start my new calendar year enjoying my independence. In this respect, I know you're right about Peter. I will try to resist the temptation to go back to him. Thanks again for the heart-warming birthday wishes.

I love you,
Pati

XI

The Nun, The Photo and
The Death Wish

The next time I see her, Mother has worsened. I hate facing more signs of her decline. Her movements are slower and talking seems to exhaust her. I never thought that I would miss Mother's self-centered monologues, but now I'd give anything to hear her prattling away.

On Sunday, just a few hours before I'm planning to drive back home, Ron, the Hospice nurse, phones to tell me something important: "We're concerned about your mother being left alone at night. Her heart is quite weak. She's at risk for a mild heart attack, or even a stroke. Someone should be with your mother around the clock. You might consider a night nurse for times when Carla or you or your brothers can't be there."

I assure Ron that Gary and Nate and I are on the same page he is, adding, "Getting Mother there is another matter."

I hang up the phone, thinking, "Here we go again." I appeal to the universe, "Please, please don't make me go down this road again." I contact my brothers who suggest we

ask Carla if she can stay every night this coming week, while we look for someone permanent. But when I phone Carla there's a hitch.
She is free the coming week, but tonight she
cannot stay with Mother as previously
planned. I must return to Syracuse tonight
because I have an interview tomorrow morning with a famous writer whom I don't dare
ask to reschedule. When I tell Mother that
Carla can't make it tonight and that I have to
leave for Syracuse this afternoon, Mother casually dismisses me, "I'll be fine. I don't need
anyone with me."

Now I'm in the thick of it. But I have to
be honest: "Mother, Hospice says that you
should not be left alone."

Mother replies indignantly, "They don't
know what they're talking about. I'll be fine.
Please let's drop the whole matter. Don't upset me with this talk."

I'm left with no choice but to make an
end run around Mother. Excusing myself,
I enter the kitchen and rummage through
her phone list. I call Nate's son Mark, the
eldest grandson, who lives nearby. He is not
free. Then I try Diana, the daughter of mother's old friend Ellen. She isn't free, either.
Next I phone Aunt Gerda, a dubious choice
given her affection for Scotch. She is tied up,
and so is her son, Alex. Eventually I resort to
Judith Danforth, the woman whose fawning
drives Mother crazy. Judith is the daughter

of Mother's erstwhile suitor, Gordon. She's happy to help out. Perhaps she's anxious to make amends for her father's Labor Day behavior.

My heart races as I enter Mother's bedroom to deliver the news. Just as I feared, she goes ballistic, dishing out hurtful remarks. I again repeat that I am only doing what Ron and Hospice insisted was necessary. Glaring at me, she proclaims, "Maybe you shouldn't visit any more if all you're going to do is interfere." I tell her that I'm sorry, but to no avail. She stares out the window, locked solid in her Ice Queen mode.

When it's time for me to leave, I stand in the doorway to Mother's bedroom holding my overnight bag. Despondently I announce, "I'm going now. Judith will be here shortly. I'll leave the door open for her. I'll call you when I get home."

Mother looks at me and replies tersely, "That won't be necessary."

I drive back to Syracuse, once again feeling hopeless about our relationship. Within a few days I receive a note from Mother:

Dear Pati,

I'm sorry about the way we parted last Sunday. I wish you and your brothers could understand that I really don't need any extra help. Sometimes my back pain and general fatigue make me say and do things that I don't mean. I hope you had a good interview.

Love,
Mother

Mother's note lifts my spirits but I can't shake the feeling of being a bad daughter, even when Mother is the one apologizing. To manage my conflicted feelings, I seek out professional help once again, phoning Sister Margaret, a nun who specializes in death and dying counseling. We schedule an appointment at my house for the coming Friday.

Sister Margaret pulls into my driveway in an old Toyota, dented and in need of a paint job. She greets me warmly and removes her rubber boots. Sister Margaret appears to be in her mid-fifties; she has a pleasing round shape, wavy silver hair and the healthy complexion of one whose skin has never been tainted by alcohol or cigarettes.

Sister Margaret listens thoughtfully as I anxiously pour out my confusion. I recite all the ways Mother drives me crazy, while including my mile-long guilt list, and my longing for greater closeness to Mother in the little time we have left.

When I've run out of steam, Sister Margaret smiles at me and responds, "So you feel like a bad daughter?"

I nod.

She shakes her head in dissent, "Well, I don't see it that way." As evidence, she points to my faithful treks to Harrisburg, my thoughtfulness in bringing Mother flowers and preparing her favorite foods whenever I visit.

"More important," Sister Margaret adds, "you showed a lot of courage by doing what you had to do for your mother, even when you knew it would make her furious."

Sister Margaret gives me a few moments to absorb her remarks before throwing me a curveball: "As for your mother driving you crazy, do you know anyone who got exactly the Mother they wanted?"

When Sister Margaret puts her coat on to leave, she suggests that before our next meeting I gather together old family photos to see if they hold any clues to my relationship with Mother.

This seems like a much better idea than Reverend Dave's scrapbook therapy. That same evening I excavate my photo albums, studying pictures of myself from my roly-poly baby period to the day I left home for college, when I struck a sophisticated pose in my second-hand raccoon coat on a hot September day. I move on to several group pictures of the family taken in various places and times and find myself amazed by something I never noticed before: in every single family photo, no one is touching!

I pause a long time when I come to one shot in particular, not because of what it shows, but because of the memory it evokes. In the photo, I'm six years old, Gary is four and Nate is one. We are sitting on a sled, bundled up in snowsuits and grinning into the camera. It comes to me that during my sophomore year in college, I went to Mother's bedroom to confide in her that I was depressed. She stared at me, taking in my words, and then shifted her gaze to the sled picture, which was hanging on her bedroom wall. Then she said, "You think you're depressed? When that picture was taken I was so depressed that I seriously considered piling you kids into the car and driving off a cliff."

Is this why I still feel like a bad daughter, even after Mother's wonderful, loving birthday letter, and her explicit apologies for her angry outbursts over nighttime help, and the sarcastic retort about life after death? Do I also feel like a bad daughter for being the family rebel, the one who's always reminded Mother of the way we really were? Worse still, have I somehow been holding *myself* responsible for Mother's depression all these years?

There is still so much that I do not understand about my mother, or about myself for that matter. I had always taken her remark about driving off a cliff as typical Jane hyperbole, but now I wish that I had asked Mother more about herself when she gave me that opening.

I begin to sleep poorly at night, sometimes awakening just before dawn with gauzy memories of Mother. Or were they only dreams? In them she is trying to tell me something, but I always go back to sleep before I learn what it is.

XII

Who's Afraid of the Grim Reaper Now?

In a carbon copy of last year, I'll be carting the Thanksgiving feast to Mother's apartment from Syracuse, and the same cast of characters will gather around her table: Sam and Mary are coming in from Chicago, Adam from LA, and Lenny from Oneonta.

Wednesday morning I place a fresh free-range turkey in Grandma's old aluminum roaster and pack it with ice. I retrieve the dented Coleman cooler -- purchased by Lenny years ago for family camping trips -- and fill it with pate, my homemade cranberry sauce and a pumpkin pie. A cardboard box holds stuffing mix, potatoes, string beans and crackers for the pate. Lenny has offered to bring the wine.

As I open my front door to leave, I glance back into the house to be sure I haven't forgotten anything. My eyes linger on the dining room table. I think of the Thanksgiving four years ago when Mother came here for the holiday weekend. My friend Arlene was among the guests that year. While she was helping me clean up the kitchen, Arlene remarked on Mother's beauty, and, in a whispered tone, asked if she'd ever had a face-lift. I shook my head "No," to which Arlene responded, "Remarkable!"

I take these pleasant memories on the road with me. But a few hours later, when I pass the familiar "You are now entering Pennsylvania" sign, I feel overwhelmingly sad at the thought that this will undoubtedly be Mother's last Thanksgiving. I long for it to be different than Dad's, when we all gathered at Nate's home in Rochester, NY. We were pretty sure that Dad had only a few months to live. He worked hard to maintain a healthy façade, dressed like a country squire in his brown Harris Tweed jacket, olive-green ascot, and tan corduroy trousers. Whenever the pain sharpened, Dad would quickly replace an inadvertent wince with a courageous smile. For our part, we avoided with studied cheerfulness any talk of illness. Death was the unacknowledged elephant in the room.

The odds are strong, given my family's model of denial, that Mother's last Thanksgiving will play out just like Dad's, yet I tenaciously resist that probability, without having a clue about how to influence a different outcome.

After I arrive in Harrisburg late Wednesday afternoon, I make some preliminary preparations for the Thanksgiving feast and then go to Mother's room to grab some time alone with her before the others arrive.

Mother looks up from the TV, which seems to be on all the time now, because she no longer has the energy to read, or even thumb through the stack of magazines next to her La-Z-Boy. She addresses me, "Pati, I was just thinking of all my things. I'm afraid I'm leaving an awful mess for all of you. How will you ever straighten everything out?"

"Don't worry about that, Mother. It will all be fine," I answer quickly, eager to move off the topic.

But Mother persists: "I want Nate and Rose to have my English silverware set. Gary and Joan have always admired my Victorian buffet so that will go to them. I want you to have my Mercury Glass candlesticks and vases and all the rest of those pieces."

My eyes fill. My stomach tightens. I stare at the plush white carpet as my mind produces an image of the three of us sorting through all of Mother's possessions. I hear myself reassuring her, "We won't fight over your belongings."

"I hope not. Remember all the bickering after your father died?"

"Please don't worry. It will all work out." Standing up, I inquire, "How about a cup of tea?"

"No thanks, but if you're going to pour yourself a glass of wine, I could manage a few sips."

The next morning I'm up early to get the bird in the oven. Mother is still asleep and everyone else is across the street at the Marriott. Around nine, I enter Mother's room to check on her. "Good Morning, Mother. Happy Thanksgiving," I chirp.

Mother glances up from the small mound of pills in her hand and speaks almost sternly, as if she is putting the universe on notice: "Well I made it to Thanksgiving. Now let's see if I can last till Christmas."

I'm stunned by Mother's candor, but I try not to let it show. I force a smile and a casual response, "I'm sure you'll be around at Christmas."

What am I doing? This is the second time in less than twenty-four hours that Mother has opened the door to honest talk, but I have been unable to step over the threshold. Who's in denial now?

Half an hour before the turkey is due to come out of the oven, I ask Sam to knock on his grandmother's door to give her a heads-up so that she'll have time to get dressed for the meal. A full forty-five minutes later, the food is on the table and everyone has pulled up a chair, but there's no sign of Mother.

I go to her room to investigate. Mother has only gotten as far as putting on her slip and stockings. She sits on the edge of her bed struggling to attach her nylons to the hooks of a faded, frayed garter belt. Just a few weeks earlier Mother would have rejected all efforts to help her, but today there is no protest. Once I've managed to get her stockings fastened, Mother points to a black velvet skirt and white blouse draped over a chair. I help her into these and, in an attempt to raise her spirits, ask, "How about some jewels?"

Weakly she responds, "You know where they are." I retrieve her pearl necklace from her jewelry box, brush her hair, apply a little lipstick and perfume and give her an encouraging smile, as if I were her coach and she were about to swim the English Channel. Mother corrects her posture and smiles bravely as I take her arm and lead her into the dining room.

After the initial greetings and well wishes everyone becomes engrossed in separate conversations. Jane is overlooked until we are nearly finished. We all seem to notice simultaneously that she has barely touched her food. Mother returns our glances, but doesn't speak, probably because it requires too much effort. It breaks my heart to see her so uncomfortable. Adam comes to the rescue, "Why don't we have dessert in Mom-Mom's room?" Mother nods her head solemnly.

I guide Mother into her bedroom and help her out of her clothes and into her nightgown. She shuffles towards her bed and murmurs, "I think it would be best if you all had dessert in the dining room. I'm very tired."

To our surprise Mother is in rare form on Friday morning. When I knock on her door to inquire about breakfast, she's sitting erect in her La-Z-Boy, studying Christmas catalogues. She solicits my opinion of a blouse she's thinking of ordering for Joan, and says she'd like to have a small slice of my homemade coffee cake.

Later that afternoon when Lee, the Hospice nurse, stops by for a visit, Mother maintains her energy, sharing with Lee the news of Sam and Mary's engagement. As I see Lee to the door, I ask her how Mother's condition could change so dramatically in one day's time. Lee matter-of-factly replies, "All patients have good days and bad days. Your mother is having a good day."

It turns out to be the last of Mother's good days. By Saturday morning she declines my coffee cake and is unable to sustain a conversation for more than a minute or two. That evening she requests that we eat our Chinese take-out dinner without her.

Later Saturday night, as I'm puttering in the kitchen, Adam comes in to ask me a question, whispering, "Mom-Mom's not good, is she?"

I stare at him, not knowing what to say. I'm caught in unchartered waters. I don't know how to talk to my frightened son any more than I know how to talk to my dying mother. I retreat to safe harbor, "Your grandmother wants to make it to Christmas. Let's pray that she can."

On the drive back home the next day I try to cheer myself up by putting on a Mary Chapin Carpenter CD and singing along with her. In fewer than ten minutes, I find my voice trailing to a stop. I'm in the grip of a long-forgotten memory. I'm five years old. Gary is three and a half and Mother has just given birth to Nate. For months afterward, I rarely see Mother. She remains secluded in her room with a private nurse who cares for her and Baby Nate. Dad hires a housekeeper to do the cooking and look after Gary and me.

What was *that* all about?

I tell myself to leave it alone. I need to relax before I head into another demanding week at the station. I slide in another CD. Mary and I resume our duets.

Only much later, after Mother is gone, will I realize that my recollection of the time after Nate's birth was the starting point on a road to other surprising recollections—memories that would lead me to an understanding of the rest of my mother's story.

XIII

Durable Demons

As the dangerous Christmas holiday season begins, I again succumb to Peter's pleas to reconcile. I've lost count of our reunions and break-ups after four years. Typically, I lay down the gauntlet when his behavior becomes intolerable, which it invariably does every time Peter decides he does not really need his meds or his therapist. He buries himself in his work all day, coming up for air only to eat dinner with me in total silence.

My efforts to engage Peter always end badly, attracting barbs like, "Can't you leave me alone? Go talk to those brilliant radio women if you must have a conversation."

After a break-up I always seem to develop relationship amnesia, caving within a few days or weeks, when Peter calls to tell me how much he loves me, how he can't live without me, how he's going to change, etc., etc.

This time I tell myself that I have a better than usual excuse for taking him back: my mother is dying. I need Peter's support to get through Mother's death. I'm like an alcoholic who finds any excuse to go back to the bottle, but this comparison doesn't enter my conscious mind at the time. Despite my gregarious nature, I'm actually a pretty private person when it comes to sharing feelings. If I knew how to tell my friends how desolate I feel about Mother, I wouldn't need Peter so desperately. As it is, if someone asks me how I'm coping, I try to appear in charge, offering up an innocuous phrase like "I'm hanging in there."

In what's become a familiar routine, Peter moves his clothes into the guest room closet and sets up his laptop next to mine in the basement office. We get lost in passionate sex, resume our witty, playful banter, cook meals together, and frequent the local art house cinema. I don't ask, but do look to see if Peter's meds are in the bathroom cabinet. I discreetly try to figure out if he's seeing his therapist by peeking into his appointment book when he's not around. When the phone rings I rush to pick it up before he can, to ensure that no one finds out that my demon lover is back.

I can no longer think clearly about Peter and me, but it's hard to repress the obvious indefinitely. Am I addicted to him? That would make me a "co-dependent." I hate to think so. No, I tell myself, I'm just in need of some TLC to help me through Mother's death. Everyone needs an arm to lean on when facing a profound loss. Besides, Peter is being so tender right now; maybe Mother's dying will transform him into a better person. Down the road, when I attend Al-Anon, I will learn to recognize this type of mental exercise as "stinking thinking."

On his way home to Rochester from Harrisburg, Nate phones to bring me up-to-date on Mother. In the process he complains about the fact that when she has small bursts of energy, she uses it to revert to her old demanding behavior. Nate describes being supervised by Mother as he was hanging Christmas wreaths in her bedroom windows: "I had to cut the ribbon on the wreaths six times before they were the right length. Can you believe it? She's dying and the most important thing to her is the appearance of her goddamn wreaths!"

I commiserate with my brother briefly before wading into dangerous waters: "Nate, how do you feel deep down about Mother dying? Do you feel sad?" A question like this might belabor the obvious in some families, but not in ours.

Nate reveals little: "Of course I'm sad, but it's pretty hard to register feelings when Mom orchestrates everything as if she weren't really dying. Despite her shrunken world, she continues to find plenty to obsess about."

Instead of simply saying, "Nate, I know it's rough, I feel the same way when I'm there," I make an almost clinical comment:

"No doubt, Mother's anxiety and need to control is a cover for her fear of death."

Nate replies, "No doubt, but that doesn't make her any easier to live with."

XIV

Christmas Approaches, 2000

Adam, my youngest son, phones. He sounds almost angry as he announces that he's flying to Harrisburg this coming weekend: "I don't want to be left out of Mom-Mom's last days the way I was left out when Grandpa died."

I can identify with Adam's feelings. When I was twelve years old, I arrived home from school one warm October afternoon and walked into a living room full of adults speaking in low voices. Mother looked terrible. Dad took me aside and said, "Gramps died this morning." No one had even told me he was seriously ill! When I asked about his funeral, Mother said firmly, "I don't believe in children attending funerals." End of discussion.

I went to my first funeral at the age of seventeen, when Dad's father died. Dad summoned me home from boarding school with a matter-of-fact announcement: "Granddad has died. He had a heart attack in his sleep." The service was short, followed by an equally brief reception. Afterward, Dad went back to his office, dropping me off at the bus station for my return trip to Penn Hall.

Death was just another blip on the radar screen when Grandma and Nana died some years later. Their funerals were also hurried affairs. I barely recall them, except for one aspect of Nana's funeral: Mother's uncharacteristic display of emotion. Mother was accustomed to suppressing tears, but in the small country church where Nana lay in an open coffin, Mother stood over her and sobbed freely as she tenderly stroked Nana's face. When I approached the casket to comfort Mother she shooed me away.

When Dad himself was dying, Mother became his border guard, fending off anyone who attempted to make the slightest reference to death. To this day I have a vivid memory of arriving at the family home after receiving the news that Dad had only a few days to live. Mother greeted me at the door in a hushed voice, "Don't let on to your father that anything's wrong. Just tell him that you're here because your brothers are and you want to make it a family affair." Her denial and control made me so angry that I refused to play along. I looked her in the eyes and said emphatically, "Mother, I'm here because Dad is dying."

Mother is now much sicker than she was just a week ago. Her voice has changed. It's grown thin, whisper-like. Her strength has dissipated. It takes her an eternity to go from her bed to the bathroom, even when I'm supporting her. Ron, the Hospice nurse, tells me, "Your mother is fading. Her spirit is strong, but her body's giving out."

I ask for reassurance that Mother will make her goal to live to Christmas.

Ron glances uncomfortably at his stylish leather boots and answers, "It's hard to know."

The next morning I pick up Adam at the airport. When we stop at a red light, Adam looks at me with his deep brown eyes and says, "This may be the last time I see Mom-Mom alive."

I reply, "Oh my! I hate to think that. I keep hoping your grandmother will live till Christmas." I'm dismayed, as I think about this years later, to realize how embedded my denial was at the time. I wish I had simply comforted Adam and admitted that he might be right.

Adam's arrival revives Mother ever so slightly. She insists on moving from her bed to her La-Z-Boy where she remains throughout the day. I take advantage of Adam's desire to be with Mother to tidy up the apartment and go out to purchase a birthday cake. We've decided to celebrate Adam's birthday a week early, hoping a little party might cheer

up Mother. Nate and his youngest son, Stephen, will join us for cake and ice cream.

While Mother naps, Adam and I retire to
the living room. He fidgets in his chair, then
finally speaks: "I hope you don't mind my
saying this, but I don't think you're being
very nice to Mom-Mom. You could be more
respectful."

This is all I need: my son criticizing me
when I'm totally exhausted, not only from the
long drives I've been making to and from
Harrisburg almost every weekend, but also
from trying to help Mother out without upsetting her. The anger in my voice is unmis-
takable, "What are you talking about? I think
I've been very nice to your grandmother."

"It's not that you're not nice; it's your at-
titude. You get so impatient with Mom-Mom
over little things, like when you tell her to
drink more water."

My anger grows. I snap at my son, "I'm
doing the best I can. You don't have to get on
my case!" My next sentence is laced with
tears, "I wish I was more patient, Adam, but
it's so hard. Your grandmother is so demanding."

For as long as I can remember, Mother
has complained about the burden she carried
for more than fifteen years: looking after five
elderly relatives who lived in Harrisburg,
four of them from Dad's side of the family.
The mighty quintet included Nana and

Grandma and Dad's three maiden aunts. It was a great deal to expect of any wife, but Jane dutifully tended to their needs and managed their care when they were dying.

In the evening, when I go in to say goodnight to her, Mother dredges up her old complaint: "There are so many things I might have done if I hadn't had to look after those *five* women." I try to listen patiently for the thousandth time as Jane recounts the "five women" litany of woes.

Mother was thirty-six when her father died; her mother was only fifty-seven at the time. For a number of years Nana lived an autonomous life, driving her own car, holding various part-time jobs and even dating. She lived in an apartment near us and had a key to our house, which she used with annoying frequency, seldom even ringing the doorbell before entering. Nana's unannounced visits felt intrusive to Jane, but Nana was a minor millstone compared to Dad's mother. Grandma was a difficult woman who had never liked her daughter-in-law; perhaps she was jealous of Jane's beauty and popularity.

After Grandma became a widow, Dad basically passed her off to Jane, which was like charging Snow White with the care of her wicked stepmother, the Queen. Eventually, seeing how much stress Grandma caused Jane, Dad agreed to pay for a live-in housekeeper. By the time of her death six years later, Grandma had gone through eight different housekeepers.

Meanwhile, Mother had also been looking after the three elderly aunts -- Virginia, Nora and Marion -- who all lived together, and died within a few years of one another. Mother found nursing homes for each of them and was their only regular visitor.

Nana moved in with Mother and Dad after she suffered a heart attack at the age of eighty-two. Jane put her life on hold to care for her mother, giving up her fifteen-year business partnership in Upstairs Antiques, and greatly restricting her social life. She even gave up her beloved bridge club, whose members included some of her oldest friends.

As soon as Nana's health stabilized, however, Mother's resentment of her self-imposed servitude began to creep into our phone conversations and soon came to dominate them. She railed against Nana's constant intrusions into her privacy and groused about her twin brother's neglect: "Paul lives only ten minutes away, but he never bothers to visit or even call Nana. That's the thanks she gets for spoiling him. Paul was the golden child who could do no wrong."

After settling Mother down for the night and closing her door, I relax with a glass of wine in the den. Suddenly a light clicks on in my weary brain: is history repeating itself? I, too, see my brothers as the favored siblings.

I, too, complain about how annoying my mother is. I remember how she used to tell me "Nana is not the sweet person you see. She can be very difficult." Only today I told Adam the same thing about his grandmother.

All day Sunday, up until the time when he has to leave for the airport, Adam sits in a rocking chair pulled up close to his grandmother's La-Z-Boy. Every time I glance into Mother's bedroom Adam is sitting in the same gently attentive posture. He is fully present to his grandmother, not talking unless she initiates it, not leaving her side even when she catnaps. I know that after Mother dies I will return again and again to this memory of my handsome, athletic son in serene communion with his dying grandmother. The once-defiant teenager has emerged as the family Buddha.

Back in Syracuse Sunday evening, I haven't even unpacked my suitcase before Nate calls to tell me that Mother has taken a turn for the worse. He reports gravely, "Hospice was just here; they said Mom's on the way out—that she may not live the week. Gary is flying in tomorrow morning. Get here as soon as you can."

It's eerie to pack a black dress for Mother's anticipated funeral and to take my laptop along to write her eulogy. Time seems suspended during my early morning drive to Harrisburg the next day. In a numb state,

I zip past one small town after another, not clocking the hours I'm in the car. When I make the turn into Mother's apartment complex I'm surprised at how fast the trip went.

Carla answers the door and gives me a quicker hug than usual, as if to suggest there's no time to waste. She reports, "Nate's in with your Mother. I know she's anxious to see you."

Mother is propped up in bed, barely able to move. Nate is next to her. When he sees me, he slides off the bed, saying, "I have to make a call."

I position myself next to Mother, who struggles to turn her head to look at me. In a low, halting voice she says, "Pati ... I'm really sick." I place my hand over her bony fingers, responding, "I know Mother. That's why I'm here." Savoring our intimacy, I just lie there beside her without speaking. Eventually, still holding Mother's hand, I kiss her on the cheek and say, "I love you, Mother." She strains her neck to meet my gaze, "I love you too, Pati."

My past reserve has melted away. Up until now I've only been able to share my feelings from the safe distance of my writing desk in Syracuse. I tell her how sorry I am that I have not been a better daughter and how much I truly love her. She looks at me affectionately and manages to whisper, "You've been a dear daughter."

The next day Mother's decline escalates. Her chest and back pains intensify. It hurts when she tries to swallow. Her body temperature fluctuates rapidly from hot to cold and back again. Her physical weakness is beginning to tax her mental comprehension. Soon she slips into a coma.

Watching our Mother die makes us all strangely restless. My brothers take frequent short walks with their wives. I decide to create a kind of altar to Mother's life atop the long white bureau that faces her bed. Rummaging through her old pine chest where she keeps her photo albums I select pictures of Jane in her satin bridal gown; another finds Mother at the Washington, D.C. Zoo holding baby Nate, with Gary and me flanking her. In another photo, it is ten years later. Mother is wearing a glamorous black cocktail dress and pearls. A photo from the 1980s shows her and Dad on a beach in St. Martin celebrating his retirement. I arrange a dozen votive candles among the photos and light them, silently uttering a prayer. It comforts me to look at them as I resume my silent vigil at Mother's side.

She remains in a coma for one more day. Wednesday comes and goes. On Thursday morning, December the fourteenth, Mother's raspy breathing has become a death rattle. Ron, her favorite nurse, arrives. I'm glad he's here.

Around ten o'clock Ron tells us that we're down to an hour or two at most. To my surprise, Nate and Gary announce that they're going for a brief walk. Joan, who rarely challenges Gary, looks at him directly and asks, "Are you sure you want to go now?" Ron requests that they take their cell phones along.

Rose paces back and forth in the sitting room next to Mother's bedroom while Carla and I and Joan sit on chairs near Mother's bed. We take turns rising from our seats to caress Mother's face, weeping the entire time. Ron looks sad, standing off by himself in the corner of the room with his eyes downcast.

Rose rejoins us from the sitting room. Finally my brothers return, their cheeks bright pink from the nippy December air. Joan and I scowl at the men. Joan says, "You got here just in time." Nate and Gary toss their coats on the floor and take seats at the foot of Mother's bed. The room becomes very still. My brothers and I seem frozen in the same realization: very soon we will be orphans.

The church bell across the street begins to chime the half hour. Just before the last tone is sounded, Mother takes her final breath. A luminous smile appears on her face! It lingers for an instant, and then disappears. I'm stunned at first, and then exalted! Joan looks at me, her eyes widening in wonder, "Did you see that? Jane smiled!"

XV

Disconnected

Ron records the time of Mother's death, and immediately phones her doctor and the funeral home. Then he dashes to the bathroom to spill the remains of Jane's morphine into the toilet. For days we've been a somber group, barely talking. Now we are all on our cell phones at once. Nate calls Mother's estate lawyer. Gary contacts Park Street Church to arrange for the service. I order flowers. Joan calls Charlotte, Mother's favorite caterer. Rose phones Mother's close friends to tell them she has passed. Carla moves around the apartment tidying up and lending emotional support to all of us.

I return to the guest room to start on Mother's obituary. As I'm pondering which highlights from Mother's life to include, Nate comes to the door and announces, "Pati, you'll have to find a place to sleep tonight. Rose and I are going to sleep in Mother's room and Gary and Joan will need the guest room."

I'm taken aback. I ask Nate why I can't remain where I am. He responds, "Gary and I have some estate business to discuss. I'm sure you can get a room across the street at the Marriott."

I may be a feminist, but I retain some of Mother's acquiescent behavior toward men. I never ask why, as their sister and the eldest child, I should not be in on any discussion he and Gary plan to have about Mother's affairs. Nate, on the other hand, is proving himself to be a chip off the father block. Even though he is the youngest child, he acts as if he is now the head of the family. Nor is he challenged by Gary, who is three years his senior.

Nate's personality is as commanding as his appearance. At six feet two, with an authoritative-sounding baritone voice, he can be very intimidating. He's an alpha male, and a talented one, as well. In high school Nate effortlessly made straight A's while playing varsity tennis and starring in school plays. Gary burned the midnight oil to get high B's and never seemed to make the final cut for a school team.

Eventually Nate became an architect and, like my father, a successful venture capitalist. Gary became an accomplished partner in a law firm specializing in civil liberties, civil rights and labor law. Dad criticized the fact that Gary often shaved his fees for clients with limited resources.

I pack my things and peek into Mother's room before I take my leave. It was hard enough to watch the undertakers remove her body, but now my heart really sinks. Almost every sign of Mother's presence has been removed. Gone are the family photos. Gone are the books that were always on the glass table. It now holds a legal pad, file folders and Nate's cell phone. Nate himself sits at the table working on his laptop. I'm so upset by this abrupt transformation, that I make a quick exit for the Marriott. I leave without saying goodbye to anyone. Over time I would come to understand that Nate was simply responding to death the way our family always has, by moving on as quickly as possible.

Dramatic reaction is always my strong suit, but I force myself not to nurse the hurt of being sidelined by my siblings, opting instead to distract myself with the work at hand. I place the "Do Not Disturb" sign outside my door and tune the radio in the room to the classical music station. Then I open my laptop and plunge into the task of completing Mother's obituary.

Even though she claimed she didn't want her picture in the paper after she died, I decide to include a striking photo of Mother taken a few years earlier. She was such a beautiful woman. I want everyone who reads the obit to see her as she was.

After lunch I deliver the obit to the Harrisburg Patriot News and then return to my room to take a nap before meeting my brothers and their wives for dinner at La Trattoria, a new restaurant downtown that someone suggested. Our conversation is strained. We don't know how to talk about Mother. Nate and Gary joke awkwardly about how she loved to be the center of attention. The women laugh nervously in response. After watching Mother dying by degrees for more than a year and a half, we're not yet sure how to deal with the new reality.

The next day we continue to check off funeral chores. All the grandchildren have arrived except for Sam and Mary, who are delayed at O'Hare by a winter storm. I fret about whether they'll make it in time for the funeral.

Later that night after I've propped myself up in bed to read, I can faintly hear distressed voices coming from the next room. I get up and press my ear against the wall like a sleuth in a detective novel. It sounds like Sam's voice! They must have made it, after all. I rush out of the room and knock urgently on their door.

Sam opens it and starts crying when he sees me. "I'm so sad about Mom-Mom. I wish I had done what Adam did and made a last trip to see her."

I hug Sam and try to comfort him by reminding him that he had a good visit with his grandmother at Thanksgiving. When Sam and Mary remark that they haven't had din-

ner, I encourage them to go down to the dining room before it closes.

After they leave I return to my novel and
fall asleep with the light on. A couple of
hours later I'm awakened by a knock at my
door. Sam, Mary, Adam and Gary's elder son,
Hank, greet me wearing long faces. Their col-
lective melancholy moves me. I invite them
into my room where they pile onto the bed
and begin to reminisce about their grandmother. Adam recalls, "When my friends met
Mom-Mom they couldn't believe I had such a
hip grandmother. She was so different from
theirs." He chokes back tears as Mary passes
him a Kleenex.

Hank smiles as he recalls his grandmother's unconventional behavior, asking me
if it's true that she once put our dog Punk in a
laundry bag with just his head sticking out,
saying that he'd feel more secure that way
during a car trip to the Jersey shore.

I laugh and nod, "Yes, it's true. Mom-
Mom picked up that bit of advice in some
travel magazine."

Sam continues to recount Jane's eccen-
tricities: "Mom-Mom once owned an Isetta --
which has got to be the smallest car ever
made. It ran on a motorcycle engine and had
only enough space for a driver and one passenger. She couldn't understand why her
friends were scared to ride in that car."

Mary breaks her silence: "You were all so lucky. I never knew my grandparents. They all died before I was born."

Adam, Sam and Hank look at Mary as if she has said something unheard of. They can't imagine what it would have been like to grow up without Mom-Mom in their lives.

The comfort and love I feel at this moment are unexpected gifts. I suggest that we light a candle in gratitude for the years we shared with Mom-Mom. The five of us sit silently watching the flame, absorbed in our separate thoughts and prayers.

XVI

Goodbye, Mother

I wake up with a jolt in the bleak light of reality: today we will bury our mother. I will never make another trip to Harrisburg to see her; she will never again visit me in Syracuse; we won't ever take another plane ride together; I will never again talk to her on the phone. I cry softly as I dress. Then I read over the eulogy one last time and go down to the lobby to meet Sam and Mary and Adam. We drive together to the cemetery for a private family service prior to the public one at Park Street Church.

At the cemetery all of us, along with Carla and her husband, form a circle around the open grave where Mother's ashes will be buried next to Dad's. Gary passes out umbrellas to protect us from a cold December rain. Nate's voice catches as he reads a passage from the Book of Ruth. Gary purses his lips, trying to hold back tears, his eyes dark with sadness. Today my brothers' emotional walls have broken down. After a few minutes of silence Nate invites us to briefly share our thoughts about Mother. Persistent themes are her love of family and her generous spirit. We are as real at this moment as we have ever been as a family. If someone were to take a photograph of us now, it would capture a rare moment of connection that will remain imprinted in my memory until I die.

After everyone has spoken, we each put a small shovelful of wet black earth into Mother's grave. Mother's gleaming brass urn slowly disappears beneath a blanket of soil. Carla spontaneously begins to sing Amazing Grace. What a wondrous gift!

At Park Street I glance around the church, identifying friends of Mother's I haven't seen in years. The church fills up quickly, although it is not packed the way it was for Dad. Because he was a mover and shaker in Harrisburg's economic renaissance during the 1970s and 1980s, Dad's death made the front page of the paper. He spearheaded the development of Harrisburg's international airport and numerous other ventures in business and the arts, but he didn't live long enough to see the completion of his pet project, the Whitaker Center for Science and the Arts, which opened in 1999.

The church is beautifully decorated with Christmas garlands and lovely flower arrangements, including numerous calla lilies, Mother's favorites. I can practically hear her telling me how beautiful the flowers look.

Being the eldest child, I deliver the eulogy, noting Mother's numerous civic accomplishments. She sat on five different boards of directors, all of them reflecting her compassion for those less fortunate than she was. At the risk of upsetting some of her conservative friends, I applaud Mother's political independence (occasionally she voted for Democratic candidates) and credit her for supporting my own political activism on behalf of women's rights. I mention Carla's deep and durable devotion to Mother and refer to Ron and Lee as angels of mercy from Hospice.

Gary and Nate offer informal tributes to Mother, recalling her kind heart and her delight in arranging family get-togethers at the Jersey shore, or "2410" (our Harrisburg house number). With our matriarch gone, I wonder if we'll gather for anything but weddings and funerals in the future.

Just as Carla shone at the graveside ceremony, she stars at Mother's funeral. When it's her time to speak she effuses love for Mother and recounts the ways Mother was there for her and her family in times of trouble. Carla concludes by saying, "She was the most wonderful person I have ever known." On the way back to her seat Carla pauses to give me a hug. We cry together in front of the entire congregation.

As I exit the church I realize how much I want to share Carla's profound love for

Mother. I am missing Mother deeply but I can't let go of all the ways she drove me up the wall. My grief is laced with guilty relief, knowing that I will never have to deal with Mother's difficult behavior again.

We have the reception at Mother's spacious apartment, which quickly fills with guests and the usual post-funeral congeniality. I work my way through the crowd. Aunt Gerda, wearing red cowgirl-style rain boots, plants a Scotch-scented kiss on my cheek and expresses her gratitude for the small inheritance Mother left her. I join a group of women my age who are wives of the current senior partners in Dad's old law firm. They all praise Mother for taking an interest in their lives. One fashionably dressed woman adds, "You were so lucky to have Jane for a mother." I nod solemnly. Now I understand how Gary and Nate must have felt at Dad's funeral when some young lawyers from his firm said that Dad treated them like sons.

I'm lost in thought when Rebecca Green taps me on the shoulder. Rebecca and I were neighborhood friends as children. Our mothers were best friends and business partners. When I ask about Emma, Rebecca explains that her mother is now in the grip of Alzheimer's disease and is unable to comprehend Jane's death. Rebecca glances toward her mother, who is sitting on a nearby sofa, smiling vacantly. What a strange feeling it is to recognize Emma's face but not see the person I once knew. The shock and sadness I feel are palpable.

As Rebecca and I talk about Jane and Emma, we discover something amazing: when we were growing up we both wished we could swap mothers. I tell Rebecca how Emma introduced me to so much great literature; and how, when I was home from college, I couldn't wait to visit her to talk about books and ideas, something I never did with my own mother.

Rebecca counters, "And I always wanted to have a mother like yours, who was more domestic, cooking great meals and decorating the house so beautifully. My mom never cooked and could have cared less about how the house looked."

What daughters of invention we are!

XVII

Dancing with Anger

During the first few months following Mother's [Mom's] death I try not to think about her. I tell myself I'm OK, and that I don't need to spend a lot of time crying because I had ample time to prepare for her death. But underneath I worry that I'm too emotionally detached: there must be something wrong with me because it's been too easy for me to move on from Mother's death.

This feeling is especially strong when I compare myself to friends who've lost their mothers: they say it took them almost a year to recover. I'm similarly surprised when I go on the internet and see whole blogs devoted to bereaved Baby Boomers struggling to cope with the loss of their parents.

On one occasion I do experience a powerful surge of emotion for Mother. On a prearranged day in early February my brothers and their wives and I meet at Mother's apartment to divide up her belongings.

When Nate opens Mother's big filing cabinet he says, "Jesus, what are we going to do with all this stuff? Every drawer is full of old cards and letters and photos."

I jump right in, responding, "Let me have them. Dump everything in a box and mail them to me."

I receive the huge package near the end of February. A cheerful Federal Express driver struggles up the walk, commenting, "This is some heavy box."

Unable to lift it once the box is inside my front door, I drag it into the living room and open it up right away. On top, as if prefacing our family's history, there are pictures from Mother's and Dad's 1939 engagement party. Successive photos document our baby days, school days, graduations and weddings. Then the cycle repeats itself with a new set of babies. There are greeting cards galore, yellowing letters in their original envelopes, newspaper clippings of our parents' numerous social and community events. Old postcards and souvenir matchbooks tour me through their many trips.

I think about the time Mother told me that I was much more fun to travel with than Dad, because he always rushed through meals and totally controlled their agenda. When we first began to travel together after Dad died, it was first class on every flight. Mother would insist that I drink all the champagne I wanted. It makes me sad to remember all this because there were so many more trips Mother and I had wanted to make together.

Towards the bottom of the box I spot a manila envelope in pristine condition. On the front of it Mother had written: PATI'S NEWSPAPER ARTICLES. I open the old envelope carefully. Mother must have saved every story I'd ever sent her, as well as every news clip about my radio show, Women's Voices.

My eyes fill with tears. She really *did* care! Aside from the wonderful things Mother wrote and said to me near the end of her life, I have no earlier memories of her telling me she was proud of me. I realize more fully now how hard it was for Mother to express emotion. If only I had understood this better when she was alive, perhaps I wouldn't have been so hard on her.

I lose it, bawling like a baby and saying out loud, "Oh, Mother! I miss you. I was an idiot not to give you more credit for caring about me and my life."

After a few minutes I rise from the carpet, clutching the envelope to my chest. I sink into the sofa and wipe away my tears.

Another surprise awaits me when I resume my exploration of the box's contents. There is an audiotape without an identifying label. I pop it into the tape deck, straining to make sense of what I'm hearing.

Finally I figure it out: it's Mother talking to a psychic! I'll be damned -- this seems so out of character for her. As I listen on, I hear the psychic telling Mother, who was apparently newly widowed at the time, that her grief will pass and she will discover happiness anew. When the psychic asks Mother if she has any questions, she responds with anxiety in her voice, "I worry about my daughter. Will she ever meet a nice man?" Mother is told that I will in time. This additional evidence of Mother's concern for me brings on new tears.

It isn't long before the tender nostalgia of that afternoon fades. My old anger is back, with all its usual resentments and regrets. I get caught up in recounting Mother's infuriating, controlling behavior; her narcissism; the way she tolerated Dad's verbal abuse; the way she tolerated his womanizing. When friends offer their condolences about Mother's passing, I thank them politely, but a voice inside me is saying, *you have no idea how difficult she was.*

In early March I confess to Chris, a staff member at Women's Voices, that I feel more anger than sadness towards my deceased mother. Chris tells me her mother was also very controlling and that she worked through her anger by reading a book called Losing Your Parents, Finding Yourself. The next day when I reach into my mailbox, there's the book. I flip through it and then toss it aside, unable to identify with it, unable to see how it could help. Despite periodic pangs of sadness and longing, I remain convinced that my relationship with Mother was a failure.

A few weeks after the Chris incident, my producer, Lucy, tells me that the station received an email from a cousin of mine who was trying to track me down. When Lucy tells me the name I recognize it instantly: Anita Banks! Anita's mother Jenny and my mother were first cousins, which I guess makes us second cousins. Jenny and Jane were close as teenagers and young women, but after they married and began raising children—Mother in Harrisburg, Jenny in suburban Philadelphia—it became difficult for them to get together. Growing up, I saw Anita on just a few occasions, but Mother kept me informed about her life, telling me about her marriage and her career as a professor of art history.

That evening I phone the number included in Anita's email. She seems delighted that I've responded. When Mother's death comes up, Anita elaborates on "how much your mother meant to me."

I don't hold back. "Thanks, Anita, but, to be honest, I had a difficult relationship with my mother. I didn't always find her as thoughtful and caring as you did. We struggled a lot. It's been hard for me to mourn her without mixed feelings"

There is a long pause at Anita's end of the line before she responds, "My mom can be difficult, too, but you must feel sad about losing your mother. I don't know what I'll do when my mother passes."

I realize I've blindsided my poor cousin with my outburst. I immediately soften my tone and try to explain: "Please don't get me wrong, Anita. I miss Mother terribly, but I still have a backlog of anger to work through. There are times when even an innocent remark like yours can set me off; it's like being under a spell of anger."

I shift the conversation to other matters. Anita and I discover that we have a lot in common. We end our chat with the promise to stay in touch.

Not long after the reunion phone call with Anita I have a profound dream. In it Mother approaches me, gives me a big hug and says, "I love you very much, Pati." I carry this dream around with me for days, turning it over in my mind as evidence of the presence of Mother's spirit. I interpret the dream as Mother wanting to make amends for her inability to be physically and emotionally demonstrative when she was alive. The dream softens my anger.

I would have many other loving dreams of Mother in the weeks and months to come. At such times I think that my anger might be gone for good. Perhaps that's another kind of death I'm dealing with. I'm used to dancing with anger, my perennial partner. Part of me worries that if I leave my anger behind I'll find myself in uncharted territory. The other part desperately wants to make a fresh start.

If I do, will the new Pat be wishy-washy and lack moral indignation, or will I simply be wiser, and more serene?

XVIII

Labored Day

In April I fly to Key West for Sam's and Mary's wedding on a beach in Fort Stephen State Park. Because they want a small, intimate wedding, Sam and Mary have invited only their parents and siblings and a few close friends, which means that my brothers and their families will not be here. It's not what I want, but it's not my wedding. When I broke this news to Gary and Nate they said little, as usual, but I could tell that they were hurt.

When I arrive at the beach, Mary's older sister is assembling bouquets on a picnic table while Lenny practices on his flute; he is the sole musician for the ceremony. The chairs are arranged in a semi-circle a few yards from the ocean. Sam's and Mary's friend Jeff, a theology student at the University of Chicago, leads the ceremony. Adam is the best man and Mary's childhood friend Carol is the matron of honor. Mary looks striking in her Art Deco-style satin gown; her blond hair is swept into a French twist. Sam's dark good looks compliment her porcelain beauty. The wedding is refreshingly simple and unpretentious.

When the service is over, Sam lets out a big hoot. I laugh through my tears. I wept during the entire ceremony -- tears of happiness for Sam, and tears of sadness that Mother did not live to see my son marry. I know how much Jane would have appreciated the simple elegance of this wedding. Mother was my inspiration when it came to things artistic. From her I learned how to arrange flowers, how to make a home look beautiful and how to throw lovely parties. We were always at our best when we shared aesthetic interests like visiting an art museum.

If Mother were seated next to me now, I'd be whispering to her about Mary's stunning gown and the gorgeous setting. She would smile back at me, nodding her agreement. I miss her terribly at this moment.

I try to imagine what Mother's reaction would be to an impulsive thing I did a few days before the wedding. Walking around Key West's Old Town, I chanced upon a charming cottage with a FOR SALE sign in front. The very next day I made an offer and it was accepted! Not long before he died, Dad had done something similar, purchasing a condo at first sight during a weekend visit to Key West. He wanted Mother to have a vacation home where the family could visit her.

We've been coming to Key West ever since. And soon I'll be a permanent resident.

My decision to move to Florida isn't as impulsive as it might seem. After I turned fifty-five I began to ask myself "How do you want to spend the rest of your life?" Part of the answer was clear: *Not in Syracuse.* I wanted to escape the city's long gray winters and its conservative politics and lifestyle.

My desire was fueled by my sons' persistent challenge to me to put my money where my mouth was: "You've always told us to be adventurous, so when are you going to do the same and get out of that dead-beat town?" But it took Mother's death to propel me into action.

My decision proves to be a good one. The only bad change I make involves Peter, naturally. The hook this time is financial: I tell myself that it will be good to have someone to share the expenses of a cottage in Key West. Peter frosts the cake with romantic talk about our living together as writers in Key West.

The Syracuse house sells in less than two months but the buyers are in no hurry and agree to let me stay on as a tenant while my Florida cottage is being renovated. On Labor Day, I decide to rent a big house in Truro on Cape Cod and invite the whole family to join me and Peter there. I want to reach out to Gary and Nate because I'm sure they still feel wounded about not being at their nephew's wedding. I intentionally promote the weekend as a belated wedding celebration.

A total of twelve family members come. The only ones missing are two of Nate's children and their families.

The weekend is a big flop. Conversations are awkward until the cocktail hour loosens people up; and, in contrast to the family vacations Mother used to organize, where everyone tried valiantly to get along for her sake, my siblings do not give me the same consideration. I suppose I should be glad that they can "be themselves" around me, as they could not be with Mother.

The biggest disappointment of the weekend is something I thought would be its high point. Weeks before, Gary and Nate told me in separate phone conversations that they were willing to join me in creating a memorial garden for Mother along the banks of the Susquehanna River in Harrisburg. They also agreed that I should be the one to plan it. On our last night together at the Cape, I pull out the landscaper's drawings, anticipating that my brothers will be pleased with the concept: a small bench facing the river, accessed by a semi-circular brick path bordered with lilac trees and a perennial flower garden.

Nate quickly studies the design, and then replies, "That's too much for me to commit to."

Gary takes longer to respond. Finally he says, "I don't think that I want to be part of this, Pati, but it's a good idea for you."

Come again? Why have my brothers suddenly changed their minds?

I'm at a loss for a response. I roll up the drawings in silence while Nate and Gary go back to bantering with their wives. Joan casts me a sympathetic glance. Sam picks up on my sadness and offers me a glass of wine. I thank him and retreat to my bedroom to release a few tears in private. Once again, my brothers and I have failed to say what we are really thinking and feeling.

Another thing becomes obvious over the weekend -- not just to me but even to Peter: I am now the target of the same kinds of jokes and sarcasm that my brothers once aimed at Mother, but in her case it was behind her back. Nate actually tells me, "You even talk like Mom." (The implication being "mindlessly on and on," not the timbre of my voice.)

By the time Peter and I lock up the rental and head for Maine, where we'll spend September and October, I feel more estranged from my brothers than ever. During the long ride my mind rolls back to memories of Nate as a little boy. The summer when he was four and I was nine, Mother often left him in my care the entire day while she was off supervising the construction of our new house. I thought it was a lark to take Nate downtown on the bus with me, though Mother never knew about it, because she rarely asked me what we'd done all day.

I also recall the way Nate would come to me instead of Mother when he had a bad dream as a little kid, often crawling into my bed for comfort. Now, it seems, I've become a different kind of mother substitute.

XIX

The End

When Peter and I pull up to our lovely lakeside rental, the trees are already coming into their fall colors. The contentment I feel in this idyllic setting fills me with fresh hope for our relationship.

Peter does a lot of his business online and through conference calls, but as a project manager for a large consulting business, he needs to fly to New York City every other week.

On the morning of Tuesday, September 11, 2001, Peter gets up very early to drive to the tiny airport in Owl's Head, Maine to catch a commuter flight to Boston, where he'll board a flight to New York.

After he leaves, I take a mug of coffee and my journal out to the deck. The morning sun glistens and sparkles playfully across the lake's clear, unpolluted waters. A single kayak moves silently along in the distance. The scene fills me with reverence and gratitude. I pull an Adirondack chair into a sunny patch on the deck, and settle in to write.

A little after nine o'clock I get up and amble back to the house to shower and dress.

I turn on the bedroom television to catch some of the TODAY show while I'm making the bed. Katie Couric is interviewing the zany British comic Tracey Ullman.

Suddenly a news bulletin interrupts them: a plane has crashed into one of the twin towers of the World Trade Center in Manhattan! This horrific sight has been captured on someone's video camera and is being replayed over and over on the TV screen. Then the picture goes live. All of a sudden another plane appears out of the blue, heading straight for the second tower! It plunges into one side and comes ripping out the other in a ball of fire!

Stupefied, I watch people running out of the buildings. Some look dazed and wounded, others have terrified, smoke-blackened faces. I feel like I'm watching a Hollywood disaster movie, but this is for real. How could this be happening?

Soon I hear a reporter say that one of the two planes took off from Boston earlier that morning. *Oh my God!* Peter left from Boston! What was his flight number? In a panic I dash downstairs to the kitchen where the phone is. I dial Peter's cell. No answer. I race back upstairs to the television. Matt Lauer is announcing that all phone service in and out of New York City has been disrupted, including cell signals. I take a deep breath and give myself orders: "Turn off the TV and go outside to collect yourself."

The lake still twinkles under a brilliant sun in a cloudless blue sky. It looks surreal to me now. The world has just been changed forever, but a heartless sun continues to shine. I move to the lower deck to be near the water's edge, where I sit and pray for all I'm worth: "Please, please let Peter be safe."

I sit there for a few minutes. The silent surroundings quiet my anxiety. Feeling calmer, I return to the house to be near the phone. After what feels like an eternity, but was probably less than an hour, the phone finally rings. I grab the receiver before the second ring. A woman whose voice I don't recognize is at the other end:

"Is this Pat?"

"Yes!" I say urgently.

"Pat, my name is Jane Conrad. I was on the same flight as your Peter when our plane got diverted to Kennedy. No one has phone reception yet but somehow I got through to my law firm in Rochester and they were able to patch me through to you on a three-way call. Peter asked me to let you know he's all right. My time is very limited. I don't know when this phone will give out. Peter will phone you as soon as he can. This has been the most unbelievable day."

I thank Jane Conrad profusely and hang up the phone, my hand shaking. I go back outside, limp with relief. Then it hits me: she said her name was Jane Conrad. *Jane Conrad!* That is my mother's name! I know it is a coincidence, but it feels like a miracle to me, as if Mother herself has gotten word to me that Peter is safe.

Perhaps the real miracle is that from this moment on I begin to rethink my relationship to Mother.

By Thanksgiving I am settled in Key West with Peter for the winter. I stay involved with the community: volunteering for Hospice, joining a women's spirituality circle and writing profiles of notable locals for Key West Magazine. I also begin to write about my mother. My initial impulse is to compose a short essay that will help me to resolve my lingering anger, but something else happens. Once I begin writing, I can't stop. Something deep inside me takes over, pushing me to write day after day. Before I know it my essay has turned into a memoir. I feel like an explorer in search of a lost world, driven to find a previously unknown link to my past.

Slowly, I begin to realize that my connection to Mother must have been stronger and more positive than I had ever allowed myself to realize. It is daunting to abandon the assumptions of a lifetime, even when you long to let the truth free you from them.

In mid-April I fly to Harrisburg to check on Mother's memorial garden. It takes a few more trips to achieve what I want; it's something Mother always loved, the look of an English cottage garden. On subsequent visits, I sit on the bench and commune with Mother, feeling very close to her. I will always be grateful to Jane for passing on to me a love of gardening and a deep connection to nature.

Peter and I leave Key West for Maine at the end of June. We're looking forward to staying in three different rentals this summer and fall, in order to sample various locations. The first place we rent, in Lincolnville, is just what we had hoped for: funky, cozy and nicely secluded in the woods. Our initial week is blissful beyond expectation. Peter even talks of growing old with me. Then his mood shifts. I question him about his bipolar meds. Peter claims to have "run out of pills." How many times have we gone down this road?

Instead of walking out the door I offer myself absurd excuses for staying. It's too hot in Key West to go back there now. I can't possibly ask my brothers or sons or friends to take me in. I could go to a hotel, of course, if I were really determined to leave Peter. Better yet, I could give him his share of the rent and tell him to get lost. I do none of the above.

By September I'm a wreck: Peter's behavior has become intolerable, except that I'm still tolerating it. Finally, one day at breakfast I tell him I'm leaving. Peter responds flatly, "Go, if that's what you need to do."

Panic sets in. My latent fear of abandonment springs to the fore. Time telescopes backward. I'm a little girl again and Mother has withdrawn from me because I've done something to upset her.

As a former therapist I'm familiar with the co-dependent dynamic that feeds fear of abandonment, but I can't fight it off. I also see myself re-enacting my mother's behavior toward my father, her persistent but futile attempts to placate and change him.

If I were advising a client like me I'd tell her that the first thing she needs to do is stop playing the chameleon to fit her lover's moods. I'd try to help her see herself as someone deserving, someone she should learn to love and respect. Yet if anyone tried to tell me that I don't love myself enough to leave Peter, I'd laugh her out of the room. *I'm the healthy one, remember? Peter is the sick one. Peter is the one who needs to change.*

I again take action. This time I ask *Peter* to move out instead of threatening to do so myself.

"OK," he says. Just like that. Within the week, Peter signs a year's lease on a house in Camden, Maine.

In the days that follow I gradually calm down. I return to Key West in November without Peter and settle into a comfortable routine, feeling stronger and happier by the day. With Peter gone, the house feels different. His negative energy no longer fills the rooms. I begin to feel like my old self. I schedule writing time for the memoir every day and begin work on a magazine assignment.

I can see clearly now that I had come very close to being devoured by Peter's illness.

What I don't yet see is that getting rid of Peter solves only part of my problem. Then one evening my old friend Sally phones me from her home in upstate New York. She's been privy to my ups and downs with Peter and confesses that one reason for her call is to ask me an important question: "Would you consider attending Al-Anon?" Sally points out to me that Peter -- despite being sober for seven years -- exhibits many of the personality traits of a "dry drunk." He's moody, self-centered, and tyrannical.

And of course, Peter is more than a recovering alcoholic, he is bipolar. He can stay *off* the booze, but not *on* the meds.

Sally herself has been in AA for years and is a big proponent of the twelve-step program. She believes that Al-Anon might help me to understand what I've been through, and how to avoid another relapse.

I take her up on the suggestion. The following Monday evening I drive to the Seventh Day Adventist Church to attend my first meeting. I'm greeted warmly and handed a "newcomer's packet."

About twenty of us, mostly women, sit in a circle on folding chairs. The harsh fluorescent lighting alters the color of our clothing and skin, making us all look slightly ashen and haggard. Each person must speak loudly to be heard over the cranky air conditioner. But what I hear fits me to a tee: "codependents" focus on the alcoholic's problems and needs, ignoring their own as they desperately try to control or fix a bad situation. The people here tonight describe themselves as struggling to "let go" of the impulse to change the alcoholic, and to focus instead on changing themselves. This is the only way to cure an addiction to a sick relationship.

I get it. What's more, as the days go on, I feel myself developing a sense of self-worth. Gradually, I find myself starting to *like* the real Pat.

Unfortunately I'm still a novice in Al-Anon when the dangerous Christmas holiday season arrives. Like an ex-con in a halfway house, I'm far from ready for life at large. I find myself stuck in a very bad case of the holiday blues, missing Mother and feeling sorry for myself as a woman alone.

While I've gained many valuable insights into myself, I seem to have lost my usual ways of coping in the process. Falling apart can be a necessary stage on the road to re-integration, but it's a helluva condition for me to be in now. Every other time I've split with Peter I've immediately gotten myself going, gotten my life going. Now I'm numb. I'm paralyzed.

Then, just when I'm at my lowest ebb, I receive one of Peter's predictably manipulative emails; and, just as predictably, I fall for it. He professes his deep love, promising once again to do whatever it takes to change. He reports that he's back on his meds, he's faithfully going to therapy, he's attending AA meetings every single day. The next afternoon I receive a dozen roses with a card that says, "I will love you forever. Peter." Like the song says, smoke gets in your eyes. Everything I have learned about co-dependency goes up in that smoke.

This time, however, it is more than Peter's charm that seduces me. I'm hooked by the greatest temptation of all: POSSIBILITY. This is like no previous offer of reconciliation; the dramatic changes Peter has *already* made go beyond anything he's attempted before. We talk several times a day on the phone and make plans for a romantic reunion in New York City on New Year's Eve. I'm intoxicated with hope.

My sons and daughter-in-law, as well as my ex-husband, come to Key West that Christmas of 2002. Wanting to create the feeling of family now that their grandmother is gone, and because the boys told me they felt bad about their father being alone on Christmas, I've invited Lenny to join us. He is clearly delighted to be here.

The day after Christmas Adam overhears me talking to Peter on the phone. (Like any lapsed addict, I've kept my reunion plans a secret.) Disgusted, Adam reports his discovery to Sam. Both sons are on my case, but I insist, "This time it really *will* be different. Peter is making big changes. He's not the person he used to be."

Sam and Adam roll their eyes in unison as Sam curtly replies, "How many times have we heard *that?*"

On New Year's Eve I'm back in winter clothes on a plane headed for Manhattan, flush with expectation. When I arrive at our old haunt, the Washington Square Hotel, Peter is standing outside shivering. My heart skips a beat: I had almost forgotten how handsome he is. Today Peter is perfection in his black cashmere topcoat, which compliments his sea-blue eyes and sexy Nick Nolte look. Spotting my cab, he races to open the door. We kiss passionately.

The weekend is paradise. Swept up in our grand illusions, we talk about a shared future together: we'll divide our time between Key West and Maine; Peter will look for a condo in Portland that we can buy to-

gether. 2003 will be the best year of our lives -
- our spirits are positively effervescent!

In February, we find a wonderful one-
bedroom apartment in an old brownstone in
the heart of Portland's historic district. It has
ten-foot ceilings, long, elegant windows, and
three fireplaces. I think of Jane and how she
would love this place. Peter and I make an offer on the condo. It's accepted. The closing
will not be until May, but Peter decides to abandon his rental property the first of March in
order to be with me in Key West.

There is a big red flag planted in this decision, because it means that the therapy Peter had so recently begun will cease when he
comes to Florida; but by now I am in full addiction mode again, color blind to red.

By the time Peter arrives in Key West his
behavior is already deteriorating. When I become active with a local peace group protest-
ing the imminent possibility of a US invasion
of Iraq, Peter makes fun of my involvement.
He grows jealous of the time I spend with my
women friends and disparages my writing
for Key West Magazine, pronouncing it a
"waste of time" because "it's not a real magazine."

After we move into our Portland condo
in May, Peter works non-stop unpacking
boxes, hanging pictures and moving furniture
around to achieve just the right placements.
Physical labor always puts him in a good

frame of mind. We are like a pair of honeymooners settling into our first real home together. Our language is playful, our lovemaking intense, and conflict is at a minimum.

But as May turns to June on our kitchen calendar, Peter turns, too. He's indifferent, detached, and even nasty. To cope, I return to Al-Anon meetings, and, remembering that Peter spoke favorably of the Maine therapist he had seen a few times the previous fall, I ask him if he's willing to make an appointment with her for couple's therapy. Grudgingly, he agrees.

I like this therapist at once. Margaret is warm, bright, and direct. When she questions Peter about our relationship he responds, "I don't know how I feel about Pat. I'm not sure if I love her. Commitment? It depends on what you mean by commitment. Am I committed to Pat in the conventional way? I suppose not."

I sit in silence and stare at Margaret's worn oriental rug, until she addresses me: "Pat, how does it make you feel when you hear Peter talk like this?"

Like shit, I want to say, but instead I opt for decorum, "Pretty discouraged. I don't see how there's any hope for us if Peter can't commit to me."

Margaret looks at Peter intensely as if she is willing him to respond to me, but he doesn't open his mouth. Finally she puts it to him, "So Peter, what's it going to be? Do you

want to be with Pat and work on your relationship or are you out the door?"

"I don't know," he says.

Margaret speaks with an edge, "Well,
what is it going to take for you to know?"

"Maybe Pat and I should come back and
see you next week; maybe I'll know by then."

Margaret and I both look at Peter in disbelief. I like this woman; and I hate having
her see me humiliated by Peter. She must be
thinking, "What's wrong with Pat? She's
smart, nice and attractive. Why does she put
up with this jerk?"

Nothing changes the second time around
in Margaret's office. Peter continues to stall or
play verbal games.

Finally I break our stalemate, "If Peter
can't commit to me after all these years,
I don't see any point in continuing a relationship with him." Margaret looks at Peter.
I look at Peter. Peter is a stone.

Adam and I rendezvous with Sam and Mary
in Chicago in July. The plan is for us to make
the one-hour drive to Milwaukee on Saturday
to spend the day with Gary and Joan in their
lovely suburban home. I have packed some
gifts for Joan because her sixtieth birthday is
just a week away.

On the drive from O'Hare to their house
on Friday, Mary seems uncharacteristically
quiet and tired, nodding off in the car. When

I mention this to Sam later, he hints that Mary might be pregnant, but binds me to secrecy until she can see her doctor for confirmation.

I'm my old self in Chicago, laughing and chatting freely with my sons and daughter-in-law. Saturday morning we all pile into Sam's car for the drive to Milwaukee. Sam and Mary have inherited Mother's Dodge mini-van. Its once-spotless interior is now dusty and littered with old newspapers and motorcycle magazines. A rubber icon of Homer Simpson is on the dashboard. When Sam parks the van, he retrieves Mother's unexpired handicap sign from the glove box and hooks it over the rear-view mirror. Shamelessly, we spring out of the van like a team of athletes.

Joan is surprised and delighted by our birthday gifts, which she opens after our lunch on their patio. Although I have no way of knowing it when we hug each other good-bye at the end of the afternoon, I will never see Joan again.

Sunday afternoon on the flight back to Maine my anxiety over Peter returns. I resolve to go back to Al-Anon, to see Margaret weekly, and to attend the Unitarian Church in Portland in hopes of making new friends. It also occurs to me to cast about for a women's spiritual circle or retreat house.

I get online. Google comes up with a soothing name, "Pine Grove," located in Tenants Harbor. The Pine Grove Web site describes a Sunday morning service open to the public. I phone for directions. The center is situated off a winding dirt road on the beautiful St. George Peninsula. The main building is a two hundred year old farmhouse, approached from the parking lot by walking across a sweeping lawn where beautiful perennials and vegetables grow in well-tended gardens.

Later I learn that Pine Grove was founded by three women who are ordained Episcopal priests. They all used to live and work in the Boston area. During periodic dinner meetings, the three discovered that they shared a dream: to start a women's retreat center. In 1990 the dream became a reality.

Tentatively I knock on Pine Grove's front door. I'm greeted by Alice, a petite woman who appears to be in her late seventies. She has bright, shining eyes and a dazzling smile. Alice tells me that I'm early but invites me to sit and wait in the "great room" where the service will take place. The room is barn-like, yet curiously cozy. The morning sun pours through bottle-glass windowpanes. Director's chairs form a circle around a low table draped with a brightly colored Tibetan prayer cloth. Two earthenware candlesticks and a large bouquet of summer flowers compliment a piece of driftwood. I warm to the room's welcoming atmosphere, feeling as though I belong there despite the fact that I have just arrived. The service begins. The group's elder, Alice, leads the service. She announces the morning's topic: *Home.*

Afterwards, the women ask me about myself and warmly encourage me to return. Driving back to Portland I offer a prayer of thanks. I've found a spiritual home.

Shortly after my first visit to Pine Grove, the tension between Peter and me escalates. He has become verbally abusive to the point that I know I must get away from him and figure out what to do next. I phone the realtor we used in the past and ask him what rental properties are available now.

"I have just one," he tells me.

"I'll take it."

Once again lady luck embraces me. My refuge is a cabin that turns out to be an easy fifteen-minute drive from Pine Grove. I begin going there on Sunday mornings for services and on Wednesday evenings for group meditation followed by a potluck supper. The more time I spend with these wise women the more I find myself garnering strength from their remarkable community.

On Labor Day morning I lie on the living room sofa and gaze dreamily out at the lake, feeling empowered and grateful in my new situation. It's hard to believe that it's been almost two years since the attack on the World Trade Center and the phone call from Jane Conrad.

As if to punctuate that thought, my phone rings. I decide to let the answering machine take the call. It is my brother Gary, but his voice is almost unrecognizable. It trembles as he speaks. "Pati, Joan just died."

XX

The Beginning

I spring from the sofa and race to pick up the phone, "Gary, what are you saying? It can't be! How could Joan have died?"

Gary's familiar kind, level baritone is now a high- pitched wail. He quakes with sobs broken by intervals of bizarre, irrational laughter. "It happened just a few hours ago. I got up early because I had to go into the office for a while. Before I left, Joan murmured, 'Bye -- don't work too hard.' She smiled at me and went back to sleep. She seemed completely normal. Those are the last words she spoke to me. When I got home a little later she was still in bed, unconscious. I called 911 but they couldn't revive her. She had a very peaceful expression on her face. I can't believe it, Pati! It's not fair!"

"Gary, I'm in shock. I'm so sorry. I'll make plans to come right away. Hopefully I can get a plane tomorrow."

Gary collects himself sufficiently to reply, "Nate and Rose are flying in tomorrow, too."

"Gary, I feel so helpless, so bad for you. What can I do?"

"Just get out here as soon as you can. It will help to have you and Nate here. I'll call you back later. I have to go to be with Hank and Bobby now. Bobby hasn't stopped crying since he got the news."

I hang up the phone and scream. A deep primal cry against the whole unfair, fickle universe. My poor brother! This is the second death in his family. His and Joan's infant son Luke died at three months of age. Growing up, Gary was shortchanged on parental love, even more than Nate and I were. Gary, one of the kindest people in the universe; Gary, the dedicated lawyer; Gary, the widower. Unthinkable.

Snatching the cordless receiver with one hand, I open the screen door with the other and go down to sit by the water for a few minutes, holding the phone to my chest and trying to compose myself before I call Sam and Adam to tell them that their Aunt Joan has died. Only a month ago we had seen her so happy, so well, so alive. I'm forced to relay the stunning news to Sam and Mary's answering machine because I don't want to take a chance on missing them. When I reach Adam in LA he has just woken up. He can barely process what I am saying.

I book a flight to Milwaukee and then push the numbers of Peter's cell on the phone pad. I get his voice mail and tell it that Joan has died and that I am coming to Portland tonight before flying to Milwaukee early in the morning. In a flash I throw some clothes into a canvas satchel, shut the cabin's windows, lock the door and head to the car. I will need to retrieve some funeral clothes from the condo.

It never occurs to me to simply get what I need and go to a hotel overnight. The fact that Peter and I will be under the same roof together is just a technicality, I tell myself. I've moved out and moved on. Our relationship is over.

Memories of Joan intrude on these thoughts: Joan, the devoted wife and mother; the smart, fun-loving woman with a memorable smile and ready laugh; the chic dresser with the perpetual tan and superb haircuts. Like Mother, Joan thrived on ladies' lunches and fine entertaining, while I immersed myself in writing and political action. Yet she and I could always find common territory to enjoy. Playful by nature, Joan was always receptive to my humorous takes on life. We loved chatting about our children, our gardens and the latest movies. Joan was invariably the one I could count on to share my emotions and reactions to family situations, if only through a knowing look.

As for Gary, he idolized his wife. He admired Joan's sensitivity and good judgment. He was proud of her popularity within their social circle, and of the lovely, comfortable home she created for him and their sons. Joan was nothing if not the appreciative spouse. Even after thirty-five years of marriage she still cracked up at Gary's jokes and openly delighted in his company.

I pass through one small town after another until I reach the turn off for 295, the highway to Portland. When I arrive at our building and unlock the apartment door, Peter glances up momentarily from his computer, but says nothing. He barely even registers my presence.

"Did you get my message about Joan?" I ask,

"Yes, I couldn't believe it."

I tell Peter matter-of-factly that I'm sleeping here tonight, and walk past him to the bedroom to decide what clothes to pack.

Peter continues to pitch his voice from the living room, "Do you think I should go to the funeral? I always liked Gary and Joan, but I can't leave until Wednesday."

"That's OK. The funeral's not till Thursday. I could use some support." My superego reacts in alarm: *Why are you asking for emotional support from a man you've dumped?*

That night Peter and I go out to dinner, managing civil, impersonal talk. We never touch, but I'm aware that Joan's death has made me long for comfort from the better Peter I used to know, to have that Peter put his arms around me now. I manage to show this wish the door, but it continues to linger just outside in the cold.

Never in a million years would I have predicted that the next family funeral would be for Joan. If her eighty-eight year old mother or my elderly Aunt Gerda had died suddenly, that would have been a surprise, but not against the actuarial odds. Only a few weeks ago we had sung Happy Birthday to a youthful-looking Joan on her sixtieth birthday. Now we were singing hymns at her funeral.

Shock and disbelief pervade the service. When the congregation sings Amazing Grace, Gary unselfconsciously wails out loud. In the receiving line after the service, the grieving widower, usually so self-contained, so private, stands at the head of the reception line welcoming hugs, holding tightly each person who embraces him.

Later that night, after the last of the guests have left the reception at Gary's home, he walks alone outside, going deep into the huge backyard lot. His cries trail back into the living room through the open windows, alerting Hank and Bobby to their father's pain. They rise simultaneously and head for the patio door. Soon the two brothers are huddled with their father on the lawn. I stand at a distance on the patio. It is too dark to see anything but a vague outline of the grieving trio against the black, starless night, suggesting that they could fade into its embrace at any moment, to join a wife and mother in eternity.

I know that I have never felt grief like theirs. While I'm now in a place where I can mourn deeply for Mother, and do miss her terribly at times, I cannot even imagine what it is like for a family to suddenly lose a much younger parent or spouse. Mother's death did not destroy my everyday life but Joan's death has shattered Gary's world. I know that he cannot imagine life without her. Hank and Bobby are now grown up but not entirely on their own. Hank happened to be staying with his parents when his mother died. He was asleep in the house on that terrible Labor Day morning. For months after the funeral Nate and I worry about Gary and his sons, but especially about our brother.

The morning after the funeral, as I lie in bed thinking about Joan, a thought I had during the service again pushes itself to the front of my mind. "What if it had been I instead of Joan who died? How would I have felt in my last moments, knowing that I had chosen to live my final years on earth with a man like Peter?

Inexplicably, I am suddenly able to *envision* myself being truly happy without Peter in my life. It's as if some kind of spell has been magically broken. The image in my head is powerful. I like what I see. For the first time ever, I find myself actually *wanting* to leave Peter, not just *knowing* that I should.

This realization astounds me. I leap out of bed. I could dance for joy! *If Joan had to die,* I think to myself, at least one good thing will come from this tragedy: the death of my relationship with Peter and the beginning of a new life for me. I wish that I could tell Joan what she has done for me. Silently, I send this sentiment into thin air, as if her spirit might be hovering nearby to receive it. I would like to think that it is.

Empowered by my epiphany, I inform Peter that he must move out of the condo in Portland. He casts me a solemn, anguished look. It is as clear to Peter as it is to me that this time I actually mean it.

During the days that follow, I keep thinking of my mother's words in her final birthday letter: "Remember, Pati, you are a self-made woman. You have so much." I finally get it: I alone have the power to make myself happy. I alone have the power to change my life.

Less than two weeks after Joan's death and Peter's departure, I've settled into a happy routine: writing the memoir in the morning, enjoying the outdoors every afternoon, attending Al-Anon meetings on Mondays and Fridays and Pine Grove meetings on Sundays. As another birthday approaches, I think ruefully to myself that maybe I am finally growing up.

One fine fall morning, my mind wanders as I sit at my keyboard; a wonderful idea pops into my head! I decide to submit a proposal to Pine Grove offering to become "the world's oldest living intern" next summer. To my delight, the community accepts my offer immediately.

Walking along the beach in Key West, not long after my return in November, I encounter Peter. For a moment -- but only a moment -- his sheer good looks strike a chord in me. We exchange polite remarks. He tells me he's living with his son on the son's boat, except for periodic trips to Maryland, where he has new clients. As I begin to take my leave of him Peter says he misses me and asks if we can have dinner sometime. The old Pat would have succumbed to Prince Charming. The new Pat does not. I tell him firmly that I don't want to see him *at all*. Peter storms off without another word. The next morning I receive an angry email from him. I delete it without replying. I want nothing to do with this man.

Peter will not be brushed off so easily. A few weeks later, while I'm sitting on my front porch reading the Sunday New York Times, he walks through my front gate. He appears crest-fallen and tells me tearfully how very sorry he is. He "wants it all back."

Peter's mood changes abruptly from contrite to chipper as he begins to talk about his new psychiatrist. The new guy, Peter tells me, has concluded that there's nothing wrong with him, that he's capable of a mature relationship. Rather, it is *I* who failed Peter, by not giving him the "understanding" he needed.

My blood is boiling but I am not about to lose control. I tell Peter to leave. He resists. I become a little anxious, thinking I might have a stalker on my hands. I tell him again to go. Finally, he does. I move inside and deadbolt the door.

I feel closer to Mother now than when she was alive, except for that last wonderful morning when we spoke our goodbyes. I keep a photo of her beside my computer, talking through everyday problems as if she were actually sitting across from me. I tell Mother how good it feels to have reclaimed my life, and ask her for help when I'm stuck with my writing. Jane becomes my muse.

The memoir rolls merrily along, at least for a while. Then I'm stuck. I can't write. For awhile I force myself to stick to my schedule, but when I reread what I've written, I know I've been spinning my wheels. I have begun to sleep poorly again, waking up before dawn, wrapped in a fog of vaguely disturbing memories.

One day, during a long-distance phone visit with my friend Raquel, who is also a writer, she asks me how the memoir is going.

"It's *not*. I'm totally blocked and I can't figure out why. Peter is history and thing's are great with my sons. I've confronted so many painful memories during the past two years writing about my family that I can't imagine there's anything left to deal with on that front."

"How are your brothers?"

"Gary and I are closer than ever. And Nate's daughter told me that when she and her father visited Mother's memorial garden in Harrisburg, Nate remarked, 'This is lovely. I just wasn't ready to be a part of it when Pati proposed the idea.'"

"That's great to hear." Raquel pauses, then says, "Pat, there's something that has always puzzled me about your mother."

"Really? What?"

"You once told me that she never sent you to kindergarten, even though it was required before you could get into first grade."

"That's right."

"Well, you never said why your mother didn't enroll you."

"It's pretty simple, really. Mother didn't know that kindergarten was required until she took me to register for first grade. For years afterward she enjoyed telling the story of her persistence in getting the school to relent, invariably adding at the end, 'If that principal had three little children to take care of like I did at the time, she'd have known it was impossible for me to get you to school when you were five.'"

Raquel says, "So Nate was already born by then?"

Something disquieting begins to bubble up in my mind. "Right, when I was ready for kindergarten, Nate was a newborn."

"So that must have been a factor, too."

"Yes, and there's something else, Raquel: after Nate was born, he and my mother were shut off in her bedroom for a couple of months with a baby nurse. Obviously, that had something to do with her not registering me for school."

A related memory suddenly returns. I begin to weep. Raquel tries to console me and apologizes for being the catalyst for this fresh pain.

"No, it's OK, I need to get this out."

I tell my friend something that Aunt Gerda confided to me a long time ago, regarding the time after my *own* birth. Apparently, whenever she came to see Mother in those early weeks and months of my infancy, Gerda was alarmed to see the way her sister-in-law ignored me, rarely picking me up, even when I cried. So Gerda herself came by as often as she could to help take care of me.

"Then, when Gary was born less than two years later, Dad hired a nurse to help out, just as he later did when Nate was born. The nurse virtually lived upstairs with Jane and baby Gary. For weeks I rarely even saw Mother. This time, instead of Aunt Gerda, it was the next-door neighbors who helped out. Dad brought me to their house before he left for work each day and picked me up when he came home in the evening."

"Did you ever learn what the problem was?"

"Aunt Gerda told me that Mother suffered from the 'baby blues' after each of us was born; but doesn't every new mother suffer some measure of postpartum depression?"

Raquel concurs, "I remember being unimaginably happy in the days after our two kids were born, and then waking up sobbing for no reason about a week later. The doctor told me it was par for the course, due to the big post-partum hormone drop; and it didn't last for long."

"I had the baby blues, too, but I never ignored my newborn sons or languished in my boudoir for weeks on end."

Something else comes back to me: "Raquel, I don't think I've ever told anyone this, but when Nate was still an infant and I was barely six, Mother put me in charge of his nighttime feedings. She would wake me up and put my baby brother and his bottle in bed with me. I'd return him to his crib afterwards. It made me feel very grown up at the time, just as I felt later on, during the summer when I was nine and Nate was four, and Mother left him in my charge while she supervised the construction of our new house."

After Raquel and I say goodbye I begin to wonder: *could Mother have suffered from postpartum psychosis,* not just a bad case of the baby blues? Or did she simply lack normal maternal instincts? Either way, it is hard to face the fact that my own Mother was unable to love and nurture me when I was an infant.

A few days later, I'm sitting on my front porch reading -- or trying to read -- but my mind keeps slipping into worry mode. I tell myself to go to the beach. It always restores me. But I can't summon the energy. Dredging up those scenes from my childhood has left me depressed. I've shut down.

What I do find helpful is remembering the wise advice of Alice, the Pine Grove elder: "Learn to let go, Pat. Life is all about letting go. You think too much, my dear."

Alice's words have a healing effect on me. I go inside and put on my favorite Carlos Nakai flute tape, kick off my sandals and stretch out on the sofa, resting my head on a throw pillow. For the first time in weeks, I am able to lose myself in a deep, peaceful sleep.

When I awake, it is dark. I'm not only rested, I'm back on track. I can see the road ahead clearly for the first time in weeks. The wrenching memories are still there, but I'm no longer afraid of them. Other, more positive scenes from the past begin to replay in my head. I grab a notepad to be sure they don't escape me.

My first memory, oddly enough, is not about my mother, but my father. It takes me back to a happy scene from childhood. *What is this all about?* I quickly remind myself: *Don't analyze. Experience.*

I allow myself to recapture the joy I felt seeing my father arriving at the end of each day to pick me up from the neighbors' house in the months after Gary was born. No matter how tired he was, once we got home he'd put down his brief case and take time to have a little tea party with me. I'd laugh at the way he looked, sitting in one of the tiny "dining room chairs" at the little table in my room, as I poured him a miniature cup of imaginary tea from my toy teapot.

When I was older, Dad listened attentively to my junior high school speeches and offered tips culled from his years of public speaking. During this same period he helped me with articles I wrote for the school newspaper. When I was in college, I was next in line for Dad's favorite novels after he finished reading them. And how could I have forgotten how proud Dad was of me when I was awarded a full scholarship to the School of Social Work at the Catholic University of America in Washington DC.

This memory triggers another from my college days. It is not a happy one. But I don't panic. I tell myself that I wouldn't be recalling it now if I couldn't handle it:

One year, when I was home in Harrisburg during spring break, Mother confided to me that as a high school student she had suffered a "nervous breakdown."

It would not be her last.

Mother never explained her high school collapse, but I think it's safe to conclude that being a victim of sexual abuse had to be a factor.

Mother had a second breakdown a few months before her wedding. She told me it was due to rapid weight loss, but brushed off my questions about what led her to become so thin so fast. All she would say is that her condition was so serious that her grandmother took her to Florida to nurse her back to health.

Then, just six months into her marriage, Mother broke down once again. Because she and Dad could not yet afford their own place, they had moved in with his parents after the honeymoon. All four lived in my grandparents' house about forty-five minutes from Harrisburg. Dad would commute to work from there each morning, leaving Mother stranded with her new mother-in-law, and with little to do all day.

In addition, Grandma was a very possessive woman when it came to her son. She openly displayed her jealousy and resentment of Jane, making Mother so miserable that it's no wonder she crumbled once again.

I was not surprised when I learned about the way Grandma treated Jane back then, because she acted the same way toward Mother while I was growing up.

After this third nervous collapse Jane went to Philadelphia to stay with her adventurous and loving Aunt Clara. Mother rallied once more and reunited with Dad. They moved into their own apartment at last, and began their real life together, more than a year after their wedding day.

Not until I came along two years later did Mother suffer what I now realize was surely another breakdown, followed by similar depressive episodes after Gary and Nate were born. *Poor Mother! Poor All of Us!*

The good news in all of this sadness is that Mother did not lack normal instincts or willfully neglect her children. By hiring baby nurses Dad may well have enabled her to remain at home instead of having to be hospitalized for depression. It is to his credit that he stood by Mother through those terrible years.

My parents were products of a time when most people didn't think in terms of families being "dysfunctional." Going to a psychiatrist was for "crazy" people. I can never excuse Dad's rages or his womanizing, but without the tools to understand himself and his own family influences, much less Mother's, he coped through anger and infidelity. Mother coped by losing herself in home decorating and ironclad denial, carefully maintaining the beautiful façade of a flawless family.

What amazes me now is that, without the aid of psychotherapy or psychotropic meds, Mother was somehow able to survive the ravages of childhood sexual abuse. Despite her depression and her difficulty engaging others emotionally, she was able to reach out to me when it really mattered. She never once criticized me for divorcing Lenny. She was totally supportive when I had my abortion, even though abortion was an unthinkable choice among her social circle. She lent me moral support when I was a single mother. She told me over and over that I deserved better than Peter. Mother had been genuinely proud of my accomplishments all along. Most of all, she was able to fully articulate her love for me before she died.

My old anger is gone. My forgiveness is complete. The relief and joy I feel are indescribable. I can finally and fully reclaim the best things about our life together instead of re-running that scratchy old movie about "The Woman Who Ruined My Life." My new mother story is booked for an unlimited run.

Christmas of 2003 is a happy occasion. Lenny and I will soon become grandparents! Mary is now seven months pregnant and cannot fly, so Adam and Lenny and I will have Christmas with her and Sam in Chicago.

The entire time in Chicago is a pleasant one. Any bickering is playful, never contentious. Lenny observes that our children are now hosting *us* for the holidays and that we are about to add another generation to our family. We exchange solemn glances as if to say that "only yesterday" *we* were the expectant parents.

Lenny and I have become the very model of a post-modern divorced couple. We've come a long way since the early days after our split. For that matter we've come a long way since Jane's death. Lenny's presence had irritated me during the terrible year when mother lay dying. His flute playing at the river seemed inane. His needling remarks drove me up the wall, as they always had.

But now, here I am, four years after that last sad Christmas with Mother, sitting beside Lenny in the home of our son and daughter-in-law on another Christmas Day, conversing good-naturedly with him, enjoying our children together, and looking forward to our family's future.

As Lenny and I clean up the kitchen after Mary's wonderful Christmas dinner, I think of the year to come: a new grandchild, the memoir, my internship at Pine Grove, and a year without Peter in my life. It's an incredibly liberating feeling, unmarred by the old ambivalence.

Peter may be out of mind, but he is not out of sight. I run into him a few more times in Key West during the early weeks of the new year. Each time he tries to initiate conversation. Each time I refuse to talk to him. He has not appeared at my doorstep again. Then, when Valentine's Day is nigh, Peter again tries to make contact. He dispatches one of his rambling emails, proclaiming his desperate desire to reunite, assuring me that he'll do anything, *anything* to make it happen -- he'll go to couple's therapy; he'll *marry* me! I continue to hold my ground. In a curt email, I tell Peter that we are history. About a month later he emails that he's joined an online dating service and is seeing two highly accomplished women. I am not even tempted to reply.

On the morning of February 18, 2004, Sam phones to say that Mary is in labor. She has actually walked from her office to the hospital! A few hours later he calls again. His exuberant voice pours into my receiver: "You have a granddaughter!" I can picture Sam's wide smile as he looks down at his beautiful wife and brand new baby girl. Joyful tears run down my face and escape into the mouthpiece of the phone. Sam ticks off the statistics: "She's long but tiny: twenty inches, five pounds and five ounces. Mary is fine. She's nursing the baby right now. I'll hold the phone to her ear so you can talk."

In an exhausted but euphoric voice, Mary reports that she had a quick labor. When I ask about names, she responds, "We're going to call her Jane."

About the Author

Patricia Taub parlayed her expertise as a family therapist into a popular advice column called Coping, which ran for eight years in the Syracuse Herald Journal. In 1998 she created a new public radio show, Women's Voices, for the NPR affiliate in Syracuse. With Taub as host and chief writer, the program won its first Clarion Award. Patricia Taub was a presenter at the UN Women's Conference in Beijing in 1995, and in 2001 received an Award of Honor from NOW for her work on behalf of women in Syracuse. Patricia Taub lives in Portland, Maine, where she remains a community activist and writer. She and her former husband share family holidays with their two sons and daughter-in-law and their two grandchildren.